Preserving Critical Thinking in a Time of Pervasive AI

A rigorous, evidence-based pedagogical foundation for educators who wish to help students maintain and cultivate their critical thinking skills in the age of generative AI.

This book provides an important overview of the cognitive impacts of offloading intellectual labor to AI and defines and probes key concepts such as critical thinking, AI literacy, and metacognition. It contextualizes the challenge faced by educators by mapping the global state of AI literacy integration across K-12 and higher education, identifying how and where AI literacy is being taught, and where it is currently missing. This book reflects on best practices and evidence-based research from around the globe, providing educators with specific and actionable methods to help their students gain the skills, motivation, and habits of mind to use AI more selectively and avoid offloading their cognitive capabilities. It also explores strategies for knowledge transfer and retention, features insights from diverse critical thinkers, and provides educators with guidance on designing "AI-resilient" assignments and assessments and integrating education-focused AI models that effectively incentivize critical thinking and learning.

This book is essential reading for educators—teachers, professors, and librarians—currently grappling with the challenge of preserving critical thinking in an age of pervasive AI and will be particularly useful to those teaching information literacy, media literacy, and digital literacy.

Robert I Berkman is Assistant Professor at the School of Media Studies, The New School, New York, USA. He is the founder and editor of *The Information Advisor's Guide to Internet Research*. He has authored several books on research, technology, and media ethics and has served as the Outreach Business Librarian at the University of Rochester. Berkman has presented on disinformation, media ethics, and research technology trends for the European Journalism Centre, the Special Libraries Association, and other universities, institutes, and companies. He earned his MLIS and an MA in Journalism, and is presently pursuing a PhD in Library and Information Science at Western University (London, ON).

Preserving Critical Thinking in a Time of Pervasive AI

A Guide for Educators

Robert I Berkman

Routledge
Taylor & Francis Group
NEW YORK AND LONDON

First published 2027
by Routledge
605 Third Avenue, New York, NY 10158

and by Routledge
4 Park Square, Milton Park, Abingdon, Oxon, OX14 4RN

Routledge is an imprint of the Taylor & Francis Group, an informa business

Library of Congress Cataloging-in-Publication Data
Names: Berkman, Robert I. author
Title: Preserving critical thinking in a time of pervasive AI : a guide for educators / Robert I. Berkman.
Description: Abingdon, Oxon ; New York, NY : Routledge, 2027. | Includes bibliographical references and index.
Identifiers: LCCN 2026029660 (print) | LCCN 2026029661 (ebook) | ISBN 9781041297321 hardback | ISBN 9781041297338 paperback | ISBN 9781003770978 ebook
Subjects: LCSH: Critical thinking—Study and teaching | Learning | Artificial intelligence—Social aspects | Artificial intelligence—Educational applications
Classification: LCC LB1590.3 .B467 2027 (print) | LCC LB1590.3 (ebook)
LC record available at https://lccn.loc.gov/2026029660
LC ebook record available at https://lccn.loc.gov/2026029661

ISBN: 978-1-041-29732-1 (hbk)
ISBN: 978-1-041-29733-8 (pbk)
ISBN: 978-1-003-77097-8 (ebk)

DOI: 10.4324/9781003770978

Typeset in Times New Roman
by codeMantra

To my granddaughter, Ida.

With the hope that she and her generation discover a deep love of learning, inspiring meaningful engagement with the world that awaits them

Contents

Preface

When OpenAI introduced ChatGPT in late 2022, it was only a matter of weeks before this newly available form of Artificial Intelligence (AI) called "Generative AI" or GenAI began disrupting how business, media, entertainment, politics, law, and countless daily activities were conducted. But the sphere hit hardest and fastest was the education sector.

Teachers and professors were blindsided. They had no warnings or preparation to respond to the seismic changes that such a powerful, free, alluring, and instantly available force was having on how their students could research, write, and complete their assignments.

In early 2023, I was a researcher and editor who often wrote about GenAI, primarily focusing on how it impacted libraries and researchers. I mainly covered how the technology worked, its stunningly powerful capabilities, and how, for better and for worse, it might change research and learning. During this time, the primary concerns about AI were its tendency to hallucinate, generate misinformation, and, of course, how it tempted students to do their homework with it.

During my research, I would occasionally come across a statement, sometimes made as an aside as part of a larger analysis, that when using AI, students were damaging their ability to develop critical thinking. This stopped me in my tracks, and I wanted to see what was being done about it.

Soon I discovered that, luckily, some people were doing something about it—namely farsighted, dedicated educators, many of whom were working intensely to figure out how to teach and design their classes in a way so that the use of AI did not damage their students' ability to learn. But they had to grapple with this unprecedented challenge, experimenting and looking for solutions, all the while still meeting their own current classroom and professional obligations.

What I Learned Along the Way

During my research, I made several discoveries. The first was the remarkable amount of creativity, imagination, and dedication demonstrated by the professors, teachers, and librarians I spoke with. Another was the sharp polarization between those who didn't want anything to do with AI and those who were ready to embrace it and integrate it into their teaching. But despite this deep and contentious split, all of the educators had one thing in common—a fundamental desire to help young people think, learn, and be emotionally resilient and healthy. And it was precisely because they all cared so deeply about the stakes at risk that passions ran high.

As for my own outlook on AI and education, I began this project as a pretty full-on skeptic; however, after spending months talking to teachers, professors, librarians, and educational theorists, I became more open to considering the benefits of certain focused educational uses of AI. Generative AI can spur curiosity and uncover hard-to-find information and sources (which is practically useful for research, but is very different from the effortful learning process that builds critical thinking and complex problem-solving capabilities). And so, somewhat akin to a supportive, knowledgeable, but not always right tutor, AI can, under the right conditions, indeed be a type of study partner.

But just as I began wrapping up my research, I became increasingly distressed about "Agentic AI"—autonomous AI models that can be instructed to go online independently at predetermined intervals and perform designated tasks. AI agents have proven useful for workers who want to automate certain repetitive digital tasks. But since they can (and have been) instructed to download and complete online class assignments, they represent a real threat to education, even perhaps an existential one for online classes or assignments. (AI agents are explored in more detail in Chapter 5). As I finish this book, I am much more worried than optimistic.

I also learned along the way just how confounding this problem is. In fact, because AI's impact on student learning defies easy solutions, educational researchers at Australia's Centre for Research in Assessment and Digital Learning (CRADLE) at Deakin University in Victoria (Corbin, 2025) have determined that it falls into the category of a "wicked problem," which is covered in the Introduction.

My Philosophy and Position

My perspective (or positionality) is that of a researcher whose profession has centered on the fields of journalism and media studies, who has also worked as an academic librarian and is a faculty member at the School of Media Studies at The New School (New York, NY). This background, as well as the primarily Western focus of the research for this book, necessarily limits my perspective and recommendations to primarily a Western audience.

There are many valuable treatments of how educators are addressing AI in the classroom in indigenous and other non-Western contexts; see, for instance, *Inclusive, non-Western Ethical Frameworks for GenAI in Higher Education: Why look beyond Western ethics?* by Mary Ndu, a Postdoc Fellow and an Adjunct Professor at the Department of Applied Health Science, Faculty of Health Science at Western University.

It's also useful to share upfront that my stance on technology and society is largely informed by the work of educator and social critic Neil Postman. This means that the lens I use to look at the impact of new technologies is through his Faustian Bargain framework:

New technology is a kind of Faustian bargain. It always gives us something, but it always takes away something important. That's true of the alphabet, the printing press, and the telegraph, right up through the computer. (Postman, 1979)

So, the guiding question for me has been whether a particular technological Faustian Bargain is a good one. What are we getting, what are we giving up, which is greater, and as Postman always points out, who gains and who loses in the bargain?

And importantly, if we discover that we are giving up more than we are getting, what are the powers that we (meaning primarily educators and policy makers) can take to minimize those downsides or even produce new benefits?

As you will read in Chapter 1, the brain science and learning theories are clear: there is convincing evidence that turning to an AI to substitute for the struggle and hard work that learning requires does harm the process that young people need to engage in to develop their critical thinking. My hope is that by surfacing a variety of innovative classroom remedies applied by a wide range of educators, readers will find one or more to try themselves.

How to begin? There are dozens of ideas and strategies outlined in this book, but to start, I appreciate the sentiment of Estonian educator Ivo Visak, who in a recent article on what AI is doing to learning and thinking in the classroom, opened by stating, "Doing nothing is not a Strategy" (Visak, 2025).

Technically, doing nothing can be a strategy, but it is definitely not the one for solving this high-stakes crisis happening right now.

Ndu, M. (2026). *Inclusive, non-Western ethical frameworks for GenAI in education*. Centre for Teaching and Learning, Western University. https://teaching.uwo.ca/genai/posts/2026/genAI_2026A3.html

Postman, N. (1979). *Teaching as a conserving activity*. Delacorte Press.

Visak, I. (2025, October 10). *Doing nothing is not a strategy*. ERR. https://news.err.ee/1609826313/ivo-visak-doing-nothing-is-not-a-strategy.

Acknowledgments

It took a small village of dedicated and innovative professors, teachers, librarians, and educational scholars to share their expertise, experiences, and enthusiasm to bring this book to life. My deep appreciation goes to all those who took the time to generously share their time and knowledge. My deep gratitude to:

Dr. Beth Archer-Kuhn, University of Calgary; Dr. Susanna Loeb, Stanford University; Dr. Kyle Maclean, Western University, London, ON; Dr. Lynette Pretorius, Monash University, Melbourne, Australia; Dr. Mary English, Northeastern University, Boston, MA; Dr. Matthew Fledderjohann, Le Moyne College, Syracuse, NY; Dr. Michelle Kassorla, Georgia State University, Atlanta, GA; Dr. Peter Bodary, University of Michigan, Ann Arbor, MI; Dr. George Cusack, Carleton College, Northfield, MN; Ivo Visak, CEO AI Leap Foundation, Tallinn, Estonia; Dr. Kari Kivinen, European Intellectual Property Office; Dr. Kevyn Collins-Thompson, University of Michigan, Ann Arbor, MI; Dr. Laura Morrison, Ontario Tech University, Oshawa, ON; Dr. Lauren Himbault, University of Manitoba, Winnipeg; Dr. Linda Nilson, Founding Director of the Office of Teaching Effectiveness and Innovation (OTEI) at Clemson University; Dr. Margaret Bearman, Centre for Research Assessment and Digital Learning, Deakin University, Victoria, Australia; Dr. Marsha Lovett, Carnegie Mellon University, Pittsburgh, PA; Dr. Michael Johnston, New Zealand Initiative, Wellington NZ; Dr. Michelle Miller, Northern Arizona University; Nazreen Beaulieu, University of Saskatchewan; Dr. Perry Samson [Emeritus] University of Michigan, Ann Arbor, MI; Dr. Pia Kiikeri, Haaga-Helia University of Applied Sciences, Helsinki, Finland; Dr. Punya Mishra, Arizona State University; Dr. Robin DeRosa, Open Education Network; and Dr. Vincent Granito, Lorain County Community College, Elyria, OH.

A huge thank you to Carol Wilder, Professor Emerita of Media Studies and Film at The New School for Social Research and former Dean of the School of Media Studies. I am grateful for her mentorship and friendship over the past many years and for the time she took to review a draft of the manuscript and provide critical guidance.

I am grateful as well to my mom and dad for our family political and intellectual debates at the dinner table, which—along with our nearby set of World Book Encyclopedias—helped spur my love of learning. And a huge thank you to my good friend Brian Hotaling who generously volunteered to be another final page reader. His expertise in words and language was of enormous value to the project.

And to my wife, Mary, for the many hours she spent reviewing and improving this manuscript; she is the best critical thinker I know, and the most caring person as well.

Glossary

AI (Artificial Intelligence)
A technology that enables computers and machines to simulate human learning, comprehension, problem-solving, decision-making, creativity, and autonomy. (IBM)

Agentic AI
Autonomous AI systems that can independently set goals, plan sequential steps, and take actions using tools to achieve an objective with minimal human supervision. Unlike traditional AI or chatbots that just answer questions, Agentic AI actively performs tasks. (IBM)

ChatBot
A computer program designed to simulate conversation with human users, especially over the Internet. (Oxford English Dictionary)

Cognitive Offloading
The use of physical actions or external tools to alter the information processing requirements of a task, to reduce the cognitive demand. (Multiple Sources)

Critical Thinking
The intellectually disciplined process of actively and skillfully conceptualizing, applying, analyzing, synthesizing, and/or evaluating information gathered from, or generated by, observation, experience, reflection, reasoning, or communication, as a guide to belief and action. (The National Council for Excellence in Critical Thinking)

GenAI (Generative Artificial Intelligence)
A category of AI models that can generate new data (such as text, images, or audio) that is similar to the data they were trained on, rather than simply classifying or predicting existing data. (IEEE Computer Society)

LLM (Large Language Model)
A type of deep learning model, typically based on transformer architecture, trained on massive datasets of text to understand, generate, summarize, and predict human language. (Stanford University Center for Research on Foundation Models (CRFM) /and NVIDIA)

NLP (Natural Language Processing)
A subfield of computer science and artificial intelligence (AI) that uses machine learning to enable computers to understand and communicate with human language. (IBM)

RAG (Retrieval-Augmented Generation)
An architecture for optimizing the performance of an AI model by connecting it with external knowledge bases. (IBM)

SRL (Self-Regulated Learning)
An active, constructive process whereby learners set goals for their learning and then attempt to monitor, regulate, and control their cognition, motivation, and behavior, guided and constrained by their goals and the contextual features in the environment. (Pintrich, P. R. (2000). The role of goal orientation in self-regulated learning. Handbook of Self-Regulation)

Visible Learning
An educational framework based on the principle that student learning should be made "visible" to educators and to themselves. (Developed by John Hattie.)

Introduction

Hard Facts about AI and Education

The rapid arrival of Generative AI has deeply disrupted classroom teaching and polarized educators. While concerns often focus on academic dishonesty, the more fundamental threat is "cognitive offloading"—or "cognitive stunting"—where students delegate their thinking to AI, bypassing the necessary practice required to build critical thinking, evidence evaluation, and independent reasoning skills.

Framing AI's integration into assessment as a "wicked problem"—one with no simple, definitive, or risk-free solution—this book emphasizes that remedies must be context-specific, iterative, and adaptable. Despite these risks, AI offers real benefits: for students, it provides access to scholarly material and Socratic engagement; for educators, it assists with lesson planning, language translation, and personalized learning. Furthermore, historical perspectives, such as Postman's "Faustian Bargain" and ancient anxieties surrounding the adoption of writing, demonstrate that society has long wrestled with technological trade-offs. However, offloading human reasoning presents an unprecedented existential challenge, making best-practice teaching techniques urgently necessary.

The primary goal of this book is to offer practical, workable solutions categorized into two main approaches: "top-down" pedagogical strategies that redesign assignments to be AI-resistant or constructively integrated, and "bottom-up" motivational methods (such as Self-Regulated and Inquiry-Based Learning) that encourage students to independently resist cognitive shortcuts. Organized into five comprehensive chapters, the book examines current research, insights from global educators, international policy guardrails, and future concerns like Agentic AI, serving as a vital resource for faculty, administrators, instructional designers, and educational policymakers.

DOI: 10.4324/9781003770978-1

In a comprehensive report on artificial intelligence (AI) and education released by the Brookings Institution in 2026, co-author and Senior Fellow and Director of the Center for Universal Education, Rebecca Winthrop summoned up its findings as follows:

> The track that we're on is not a good one. What we found is that currently with AI implementation for students in education, the risks are overshadowing the benefits.
>
> (Burns et al., 2026)

University and college faculty, educational administrators, librarians, and teachers had virtually no warning of AI's arrival. It immediately disrupted the most fundamental matters of classroom teaching and learning. The technology changes and improves at dizzying speeds, and it all can be confusing and frightening. Educators' opinions about whether to embrace or reject AI in the classroom are highly passionate and polarized.

This book establishes where educators can examine AI in the classroom, and suggests a wide range of strategies for helping to ameliorate the major risks it presents, particularly its impacts on the development of critical thinking.

What's at Stake

It's common knowledge that since November 2022, when OpenAI introduced ChatGPT, students have been regularly turning to Generative AI systems (ChatGPT or one of the other popular models, e.g., Claude, Gemini, Co-Pilot, etc.) to complete their papers or other school assignments. But concerns are still often framed as dealing with the problem of "cheating." In fact, the risk of students turning to AI to do their thinking for them (i.e., "cognitive offloading") is much more fundamental: what's at stake is students' ability to build new skills, deeply learn, and develop their critical thinking capabilities.

The Brookings Institution conducted a comprehensive research report, *A New Direction for Students in an AI World: Prosper, Prepare, Protect*, published in January 2026 (Burns et al., 2026). The report's co-author, Rebecca Winthrop, addresses the findings in an interview with Tristan Harris, founder of the Center for Humane Technology, in the March 2026 episode of its podcast, *Your Undivided Attention*:

> *… We really found several big ways AI interferes with children's ability to learn. The first one is undermining kids' cognitive development. So, this is where kids are not just using AI to help them think critically or help them be more creative, but not as a cognitive partner, but as a cognitive surrogate. So instead of them going through the thinking process and doing it themselves…we use the term cognitive offloading because that is what people use in the literature and in the field. And in fact, I actually think*

> *for kids, cognitive offloading isn't even the right term. It's actually cognitive stunting because kids aren't even developing the critical thinking and learning skills to offload in the first place.*
>
> *So, when you assign an essay to a child, a student, they have to think through what is the data? What is the evidence? How does it stack up? Is there a side of the argument the data sits on that isn't? How do I make a persuasive argument that uses this data and have a position?*
>
> *Those are hugely difficult skills to develop and they come through practice. And if you stick in a couple sentences into a chatbot and have it write the essay for you, kids aren't just merely skipping a couple steps in their homework and being more efficient. They are missing the opportunity to develop their own personal independent thinking skills.*
>
> (Harris & Raskin, 2026)

Making matters even more complex, according to a group of educational researchers at the Centre for Research in Assessment and Digital Learning (CRADLE) at Deakin University (Victoria, Australia), the problem of AI in the classroom falls into a kind of "super" problem known as "wicked."

In the journal article, "The Wicked Problem of AI and Assessment" (Corbin, 2025), the authors cite the seminal work of Rittel and Weber (1973) that there exist certain problems that defy simple solutions, which they term wicked. These, according to the researchers, share the same defining characteristics:

> …they do not have a definitive formulation; there is no "stopping rule" that signals when they are solved; the solutions are not true or false, only good or bad; there is no way to test the solution; they cannot be studied through trial and error because each attempt has real life consequences; there are seemingly a limitless number of solutions or approaches to deal with the problem; each wicked problem is basically unique; they can always be described as the symptom of other problems; the way the problem is described determines its possible solutions; and finally, the decision maker who chooses how to solve the problem bears full responsibility for the consequences of their choices

The authors applied Rittel and Weber's formulation to determine that classroom assessment in the context of Generative AI meets those criteria and so qualifies as a wicked problem.

Since wicked problems, by definition, do not lend themselves to a single right/wrong answer, one way to arrive at possible remedies is by considering *multiple* solutions and determining which are most likely to be suitable and successful for one's own particular context. Educators can engage in trying different solutions, even with the realization that they will almost certainly be imperfect, incomplete, and will likely need to be revised and rethought (or even abandoned) in any future implementation.

Possible Benefits of Classroom AI

The real benefits that AI (not necessarily Generative AI) can provide are also numerous. For students, these include the ability to access enormous amounts of scholarly, scientific, and substantive information, and if so desired, in a summarized and organized manner with analysis of how it fits together; AI can be useful for identifying hard-to-find and unusual resources, too. It has proven to be of great assistance in helping researchers determine the best keywords to describe their topic for follow-up searches in traditional online databases. Educationally designed LLMs may, in fact, spur critical thinking through a Socratic question-and-answering process, though it is not clear, at least yet, how AI-enabled questioning produces learning compared to a process conducted by or with other people.

And for teachers, faculty, librarians, and other educators, AI has been useful for tasks like generating lesson plans, though this function is not without critics who worry about over-reliance by novice teachers who may miss out on learning how to create these themselves. AI has also proven to be very useful for certain forms of personalized learning, including creating customized assignments for students with special needs, and in some cases for producing exams. And AI will certainly continue to be relied upon as a fast and accurate technology for language translation and tutoring.

Finally, although most educators don't want students to use AI to do their writing for them, it now appears that most now permit AI to aid students with more technical and lower-level matters like initial brainstorming of ideas, assistance with grammar, sentence structure, and organization.

Haven't We Been Here Before?

A "what must be done" worry about the impact of AI technology for youth often prompts the response of: Yes, well, haven't we always had to adjust to new technologies? We certainly can't stop them, so we had better learn to live with AI and adapt, and this is the nature of how information and communication technologies progress.

Putting aside the much larger and weightier social and political issue of why citizens do not have a more meaningful voice in determining what new technologies or products they *want* to have, this "haven't we always had to do this" objection is a reasonable one and should be met head-on.

And, yes, of course, worries over what happens when a new communication/information technology replaces a human capability is an old, even ancient story. Whether the new technology is a digital one like the Internet, computers, GPS, online databases, or calculators, or pre-digital inventions like automobiles, telephones, or the telegraph, there have always been anxieties over what we all may have to give up for the "progress" that these new creations have provided. The trade-offs that these transactions create were perhaps most famously described by educator and social critic Neil Postman as our "Faustian Bargain" with technology, as noted in the preface.

So it is certainly an old story. And there were worries in 370 BCE about the new technology called writing, as expressed through Plato's Dialogue, *Phaedrus*.

> *For this invention will produce forgetfulness in the minds of those who learn to use it, because they will not practice their memory. Their trust in writing, produced by external characters which are no part of themselves, will discourage the use of their own memory within them" Phaedrus 14, 274c-275b [see: https://www.historyofinformation.com/detail.php?id=3439]*

And, in fact, those worries that we would give up some ability to remember were accurate, but most agree that the implicit bargain made here—permanence and transportability of knowledge—was worth the trade-off. Other technology Faustian bargains have a different calculus.

It is also true that for eons humans *have* been offloading tasks they had to do themselves onto external devices or technology that can do the job faster, more accurately, and more efficiently. And as with writing, we may say that some were good bargains, while for others, say social media, the drawbacks may have outweighed the benefits.

So how should we think about offloading our thinking?

In his fascinating book, *Knowing What We Know: The Transmission of Knowledge: From Ancient Wisdom to Modern Magic* (Winchester, 2023), noted British author Simon Winchester explores how humans have gained and shared knowledge throughout history, often advanced and accelerated by a new technology. But in his book, Winchester worries that with AI, we are at a novel and more existential point. If we farm out critical thinking and our ability to reason itself, he wonders, what do humans really have left?

As you read through the strategies, cases, and ideas shared in this book, keep in mind that because figuring out how to address the presence of AI in teaching and learning is a "wicked" problem, there is no single solution that will work for all educators and circumstances. It will be up to each individual to determine, based on their own context, which design choices, motivators, and incentives will be most appropriate and most likely to succeed.

For some educators, the strategies identified in this book may not be new, and, in fact, many of these (scaffolding assignments, formative assessment, engagement strategies, etc.) have been advocated for years by leading educational researchers. However, it is also true that given the presence and potential of the counter-learning impacts of AI, the need to now implement these best practice teaching techniques has moved from nice, but perhaps not necessary, to more urgent.

Ultimately, of course, this entire discussion goes back to the much more fundamental question of what it means to learn, how to teach so students learn, and why an educator has chosen their path to take on this mission. And ironically, this disruption by AI has forced many teachers who have not changed the way they taught for many years to go back to basics and consider these fundamental matters of learning anew.

The Key Goals

This book's primary goal is to share a range of educators' ideas, strategies, use cases, and practices as possible workable solutions for addressing the risks of students' loss of learning and critical thinking from AI. These approaches can be broadly grouped into two categories: educators that have designed their classroom assignments and assessments to try to ensure that AI does not hinder learning and thinking (the "top down" approaches shared by educators in Chapters 2 and 3) or introducing motivational strategies to incentivize students to consider, for themselves, the costs and benefits of turning to AI, and then helping them to make wiser and healthier judgments *of their volition* when it is best to avoid using the technology ("bottom up" strategies examined in Chapter 4).

These strategies are likely to be of value to a range of educational professional readers: notably, faculty, academic leadership and senior administrators, library directors, educational and academic developers, instructional or learning designers, and pedagogical specialists. In addition, secondary school teachers, administrators, and school librarians can benefit from these lessons as well as local, state, and national educational policy makers.

How This Book Is Organized

Chapter 1: The AI Classroom Landscape lays out where things stand in terms of student use of AI, including the rates of increase, what purposes it's being used for, what spurs how they use it, and where they see it helping and harming them. Also examined are how educators feel about AI in the classroom, and where they are most concerned. There have also been several major international research projects that have studied AI in the classroom that issued reports in 2026—their findings and implications are also included in this chapter.

Chapters 2 and 3: Voices from the Field: How Educators Are Protecting Student Thinking and Learning These two chapters share (lightly edited) transcripts of in-depth Zoom conversations with 12 educators who integrated a range of strategies to address AI's impact on their students' learning and critical thinking. The educators include higher ed faculty, professionals in Teaching and Learning Centers, librarians, and one secondary school teacher, and are from the United States, Canada, Australia, and Finland. Chapter 2 includes educators whose goal was primarily to make their classroom more "AI Resistant" while Chapter 3 includes those who worked to integrate AI, though specifically education-focused AI, into the assignments.

The educators selected to be interviewed in these chapters were selected via a few methods: reviewing educational conference programs and reaching out to presenters; by posting requests for participants on two faculty teaching and learning Google discussion groups: POD Network's online discussion forum (includes professionals from university centers for teaching and learning) and ISSOTL, the International Society for the Scholarship of Teaching and Learning; by searching and reviewing relevant journal articles and directly contacting selected authors; and from referrals by interviewees to other educators. Each interview was conducted by Zoom; most ran between 45 minutes to an hour, were recorded, and each participant had the opportunity to do a fact-check and make any corrections or clarifications in the transcript. This research was conducted from January through May 2026.

Chapter 4: When No One is Watching: Motivating Students to Resist the Cognitive Shortcut explores the challenge of how educators can motivate and incentivize students of their own volition to make better judgments about when it's OK and when it is not OK to use AI for class assignments when they are back home or in another unsupervised location. While Chapters 2 and 3 are all about educators who have come up with top down classroom designs that by default or logic steer students to not need to use general-purpose AI systems, this chapter explores learning, psychological, and educational motivational methods that can also be utilized to help students make the right choices. Covered here are teaching methods such as Inquiry-Based Learning, Self-Regulated Learning, and others.

Chapter 5: Lessons Learned and Future Forewarnings: The concluding chapter pulls together the larger themes that emerge from the strategies and practices shared by the educators in this book, The chapter also examines how EdTech is responding to AI; the threats that Agentic AI is posing to online education and what educators can do about it; concerns over the rise in "Persuasive AI;" how AI's form of reasoning may impact decision making; and the importance of considering the "Precautionary Principle" when integrating AI into the classroom.

A final segment shares how an indigenous perspective on learning can provide deeper insights on what counts as meaningful knowledge, and why AI falls short.

Appendix: The appendix provides a quick summary of laws, policies, and guidance that selected countries around the globe have passed or proposed to address concerns about how AI is integrated into classrooms in their country. Countries and regions covered include Finland, Estonia, the European Union, Singapore, Korea, Australia, New Zealand, and the United States, with a briefer round-up of what is happening elsewhere.

References

Burns, M., Winthrop, R., Luther, N., Venetis, E., & Karim, R. (2026, January). *A new direction for students in an AI world: Prosper, prepare, protect.* Center for Universal Education at The Brookings Institution.

Corbin, T., Bearman, M., Boud, D., & Dawson, P. (2025). The wicked problem of AI and assessment. *Assessment & Evaluation in Higher Education*, 1–17.

Harris, T., & Raskin, A. (Hosts). (2023–present). *Your undivided attention* [Audio podcast]. Center for Humane Technology.

Harris, T., & Raskin, A. (Hosts). (2026, March 5). AI is breaking education. Rebecca Winthrop has the blueprint to fix it (No. 128) [Audio podcast episode]. In *Your Undivided Attention.* Center for Humane Technology.

Rittel, H. W., & Webber, M. M. (1973). Dilemmas in a general theory of planning. *Policy Sciences*, *4*(2), 155–169.

Winchester, S. (2023). *Knowing what we know: The transmission of knowledge: From ancient wisdom to modern magic.* HarperCollins.

1 The AI Classroom Landscape

How Students, Educators, and Global Research Bodies View Benefits and Risks

AI has been causing seismic changes in the teaching and learning classroom landscape ever since OpenAI's release of ChatGPT in November 2022. And it's not just teachers and professors, but, increasingly, students as well, pushing back on how AI is transforming learning. As one researcher told, in a 2026 study, titled *Everyone's using it but no one is allowed to talk about it: College students' experiences navigating the higher education environment in a generative AI world*, "AI picks me up from point A and drops me at point B without me learning the journey. Then when I try to get to point C alone, I don't know how. I'm stuck without the learning experience" (Fu, Y et al., 2026).

This chapter examines where things stand in the early Summer of 2026, with the obvious caution that usage data and trends continually change, so they must be viewed in the context of this time frame. However, this chapter also reviews findings and advisories of key expert research bodies studying the challenges AI produces in the classroom, and these can be considered much more sustainable over time.

One other prefatory point. While the primary focus of this book is the use of AI in the higher education classroom, there are circumstances when it is also relevant and important to discuss usage in secondary school. Several surveys and state legislative activities surface in this chapter are focused on that grade level, and noted as such.

How Students Are Using AI

Looking first at surveys of student AI use in higher education, a 2026 preprint (Fu, Y., et al., 2026), cited researchers Fosner, Hu et al., Rong et al., and Welding, who found that anywhere from 60% to 86% of students were using it for academic work, representing a dramatic increase from a rate of 43% two years prior. Given the rate of growth, it is virtually certain that those numbers will continue to increase (with the proviso of a possible slowdown based on some AI pushback by Gen Z-aged students, as discussed further). Interestingly, Fu, Y. also found that the biggest

DOI: 10.4324/9781003770978-2

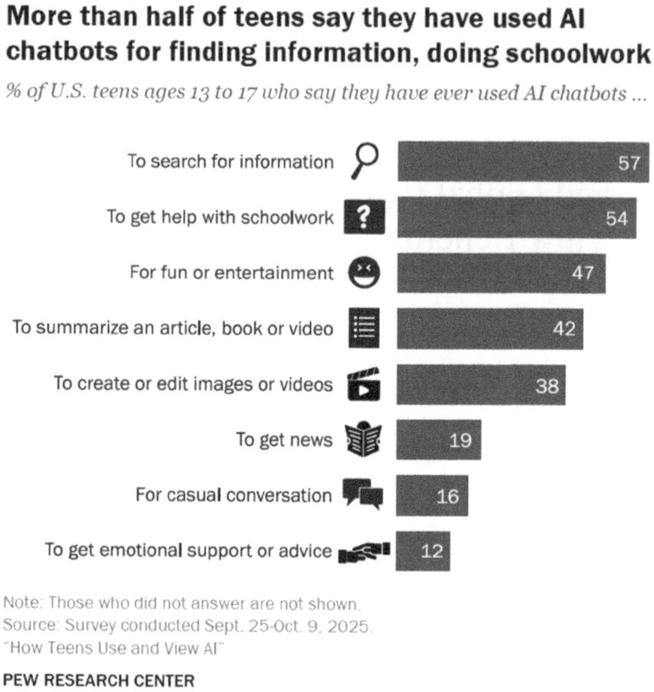

Figure 1.1 A 2025 Pew Research Survey found that the top two uses of AI by teens are to search for information and to get help with schoolwork.

determinant of *whether and how often* and *when* a student chooses to use AI is the influence of their peer group.

Pervasive student use of AI by students is no longer news, but it still is revelatory to discover how and why they use it. According to research done in December 2025 by Pew Research (Pew, 2025), of teenagers aged 13–17 who say they have used AI chatbots, the top two uses are to search for information (57%) and to get help with schoolwork (54%) (see Figure 1.1).

For university students, the Stanford 2026 AI Index Report reported that about 80% of students around the world are using GenAI to support their studies, with researching, brainstorming, generating ideas, and editing essays reported as the top uses. (Data collected in 2025 by Chegg). GenAI usage ranges from a high of 95% for Indonesian students to a low of 67% for those in the United States and the UK. The most common AI use reported was "understanding a concept or subject."

But while student usage is indeed pervasive, it is also accompanied by a great deal of anxiety and uncertainty. In fact, as examined in Fu, Y., et al. (2026), students are unsure and nervous about when it is OK to use it and when it is not. In fact, that doubt has produced what has created, for some, something that has come to be known as "AI Shame." A key reason for this uncertainty is the lack of clarity, guidance, or consistent rules from their teachers or educational institutions on when AI use is permitted.

And while still primarily anecdotal, the younger-middle portion of the Gen Z demographic, born between 1997 and 2012 (age 14–29 in 2026), is reportedly increasingly expressing anti-AI views (as dramatically evidenced by several 2026 College Commencement speeches where speakers that heralded AI were roundly booed). Their reasons for rejecting AI vary but include its expected impact on jobs, along with concerns about its impact on the environment. Other reasons for their negative views may include distrust of corporate tech companies and awareness of the harm caused by social media and digital technology dependence. It will be interesting to discover if the following demographic (Alpha Generation born 2010–2024) continues this, pushing back on AI.

Some surveys have also found students expressing a broad range of concerns about how over-reliance on AI could negatively impact them personally. For example, a 2025 survey by Turnitin identifying what challenges were top for academic administrators, educators, and students found that the highest challenge cited was "worried about becoming over-reliant on AI" and the biggest risk was "over-reliance on AI, reducing critical thinking skills." (See Figure 1.2).

Concerns included not being able to deeply learn a topic, creating lesser works, not developing their authentic voice, stunting their thinking, lessening their creative capabilities, and violating their values and integrity.

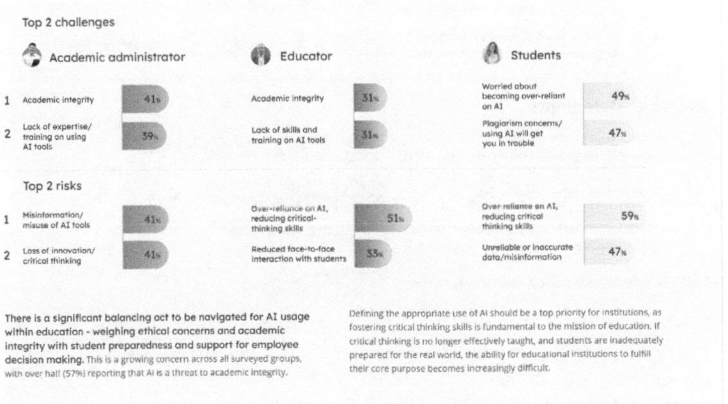

Figure 1.2 A Turnitin survey found the biggest risk students cited on using AI was over-reliance on AI reducing critical thinking skills.

In some surveys, students responded to their negative learning experiences directly. Consider this [higher education] student's comments: (Fu, Y et al., 2026)

> When I use AI, I haven't seemed to remember anything. I don't think I retained it well enough or learned deeply enough.

Objections to using AI have even taken the form of active resistance, creating a dilemma for educators who have required AI to be utilized for a particular assignment.

College Educators Are Deeply Divided

Higher ed faculty are split on the question of whether to embrace or to reject AI in the classroom, with both sides extremely passionate about the virtue of their viewpoint to the point where one pro-AI use professor told me she became actively shunned by her colleagues.

Despite this split, there is one important area of agreement, and it relates to technology's impact on thinking. On February 25, 2026, in a study by The College Board (The College Board, 2026), 84% of faculty surveyed agreed that AI reduces students' critical thinking, originality, and deep engagement

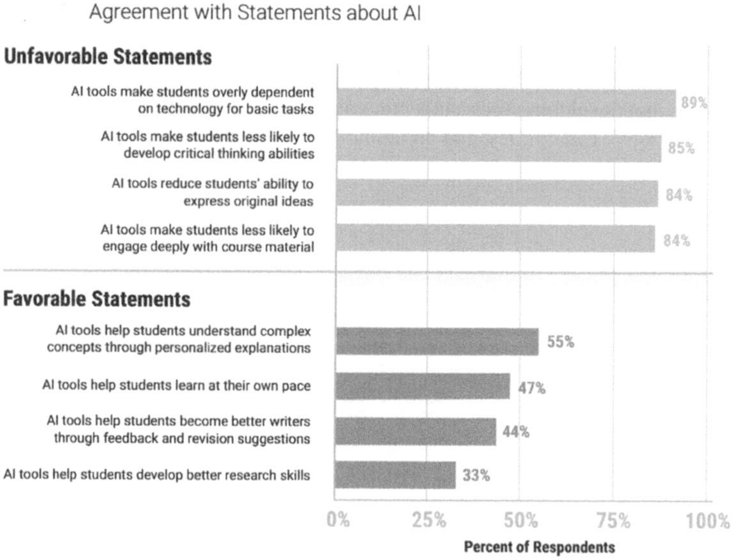

Figure 1.3 A study by the College Board found 84% of faculty surveyed agreed that AI reduces students' critical thinking, originality, and deep engagement with their course materials.

with their course materials. The survey broke down responses by the faculty on a range of areas and by academic discipline (see Figure 1.3).

What's at Stake

Starting around 2023, scientists began researching what happens in the brain when one turns to AI as a substitute for engaging in effortful thinking, struggle, and analysis. The findings of the two that have been widely discussed are noted below:

- Your Brain on ChatGPT: Accumulation of Cognitive Debt When Using an AI Assistant for Essay Writing Task: MIT Media Lab, June 10, 2025; arxiv. org/pdf/2506.08872

  This study assigned 54 university-educated participants to three groups: those who used ChatGPT to write essays, those who used Google Search, and those who wrote unaided. EEG monitoring assessed neural engagement, while linguistic and retention measures gauged performance.

  The researchers concluded that ChatGPT users exhibited the lowest neural engagement, poorest linguistic outcomes, and diminished retention compared to both search engine users and the brain-only group. Over repeated tasks, ChatGPT users increasingly resorted to copy and paste, suggesting declining cognitive investment. The brain-only group maintained the strongest cognitive activation and original composition.
- AI Tools in Society: Impacts on Cognitive Offloading and the Future of Critical Thinking *Societies*, Jan 3, 2025; mdpi.com/2075 4698/15/1/6?ref=newcanaanunplugged.org

  This study looked at how AI tool usage affects critical thinking abilities. The construct of cognitive offloading was looked at as a key mediating factor in the use of AI. The study was conducted with a UK population across age groups and educational backgrounds.

  The core conclusion of this research was that there was "a significant negative correlation between the frequent AI tool usage and critical thinking abilities. …" AI tools diminished users' engagement in reflective thinking processes.

[For additional studies measuring the impact of AI on cognition, see Berkman, 2025]

What Learning Scholars Are Telling Us

Maryanne Wolf is the UCLA Professor-in-Residence of Education and Director of its Center for Dyslexia, Diverse Learners, and Social Justice, and the Chapman University Presidential Fellow. She is also the author of the highly acclaimed book *Proust and the Squid: The Story and Science of the Reading Brain (2007)* as well as *Reader Come Home: The Reading Brain in a Digital World (2018)*, which examines the negative impact digital technology has on our ability to perform deep reading.

In April 2025, in another an episode of the "For Your Undivided Attention" podcast (Harris, 2025), she was interviewed by Center for Humane Technology Co-founder and President, Tristan Harris, to discuss AI's impact on how we think and learn, particularly for the "reading brain," as excerpted below:

> *How do we develop thinking? There are several sets of skills we want our children to learn ... skills that are analogic, inferential, empathic, and most importantly the sum of which is critical thinking... When we build this circuit-the circuit has a very basic function: the whole point of learning is to use the* **effort***...and this is what I want to say is so worrisome to me about AI. It's the efforts to build these circuits...to make analogical skills, to make inferential skills...One of the most beautiful parts of learning is... that all adds to the ability of the learner to become critically analytic about what they are reading. Now the problem with AI for me is what we call cognitive offloading, which in the interest of efficiency we can do all this faster and better if we are using these technological devices. The reality is that what we need as learners are the efforts:*
>
> *Even Emerson said "when we are braced by labors that's where thinking begins" — and all of that is in the interests of the imaginative insights of the individual. All of that should never be short circuited in the interest... of efficiency or the best grade. If we can somehow model the importance of effort and labor that's what builds the circuit of the deep reader.*
>
> (@ 4.58-7.21)

Why It Matters So Much

It is clear that risking thinking and learning in youth matter greatly. But in addition to the risk of AI stunting and harming an individual young person's capacity to learn and think, there are additional vital matters at stake. Among them are:

A rupturing in the relationship between students and their teacher. Teachers are suspicious of students surreptitiously using AI, and increasingly, students themselves have become suspicious of their *teachers* using AI and don't like that either.

The future impact on a well-functioning society. If, as adults, today's students' critical thinking was indeed stunted or diminished, they will have a lessened ability to think critically about life decisions: not only those that affect them, but those that affect their community and fellow citizens.

Ken Timmons, a UK Royal Society Fellow and a renowned Professor of Microbiology, co-wrote an editorial in the August 2025 issue of *Microbial Biotechnology* titled "Scientists' Warning to Humanity: The Need to Begin Teaching Critical and Systems Thinking Early in Life." An excerpt from the abstract:

> *We live in a time of global crises: a deteriorating environment that is struggling to provide all the resources and services we demand of it, changing climate and its consequences for the biosphere, its habitats, inhabitants and biodiversity, conflicts-divisive ideologies-competition for resources, increasing societal inequalities and human deprivations, and a youth mental health pandemic, to name but just a few. [S]ensible decisions are urgently needed at all levels to fix problems and reduce future self-harm.*
>
> *Sensible decisions require sourcing the best available relevant information, and a process to convert information into understanding, understanding into clear decision options, and the choice of a decision option that leads to an action that represents best practice. Critical thinking is the enabling cognitive process of this decision pathway, because it selects the best available information through demanding evidence-basing, seeks critical discourse between experts and stakeholders that agnostically explores solution space to find plausible options, and whittles down options inter alia through plausibility, due diligence, bottleneck analysis, cost-benefit analysis, and benchmarking filtering...*
>
> (Timmis, 2025)

> In the piece, in his discussion of independent thinking, Timmons addresses AI this way "there are several forces that suppress independent thinking, but AI is perhaps one of the most insidious"
>
> (Timmis, Sec 5.3)

Findings from International Organizations and Think Tanks

The impact of AI on student learning and thinking has been of special concern to several major international research bodies. Among these are the Organization for Economic Co-operation and Development (OECD), the Brookings Institution (Washington, DC), and RAND (Santa Monica, CA), all of which released major reports in 2026. While any substantive summary of these studies would be beyond the scope of this chapter, it is possible to review their topline findings and recommendations, particularly as they relate to AI's impact on the development of learning and critical thinking. (Links to the full reports are provided on the Works Cited page.)

In January 2026, **the Brookings Institution** published *A New Direction for Students in an AI World: Prosper, Prepare, Protect.* This 219-page study stated that its goals were to help readers understand "the current landscape of benefits and risks of AI in children's education and help them identify concrete actions they can take to leverage AI for transformational educational benefits." There is an enormous amount of detail and insights in this powerful report, but as noted in the Introduction, the report leads with its key finding: "currently the risks of AI overshadow the benefits."

AI's impact on the development of critical thinking is examined multiple times in the study. One section explores how the process of cognitive offloading is something that humans have been doing for a long time to aid memory and free up thinking space. But the authors also note special worrying factors when it comes to cognitive offloading to AI:

> AI has turbocharged cognitive offloading. LLMs, for example, offer capabilities extending far beyond traditional productivity tools into domains previously requiring uniquely human cognitive processes. As AI tools continuously improve, they become increasingly seductive to use, creating what amounts to an existential danger to learning itself. Research reveals a strong positive correlation ($r = +0.72$) between excessive AI tool use and cognitive offloading, with younger participants who relied heavily on AI tools scoring lower on critical thinking skills than their older counterparts (Gerlich, 2025).
>
> (Burns, 2026, p.57)

A March 2026 RAND report, *More Students Use AI for Homework, and More Believe It Harms Critical Thinking: Selected Findings from the American Youth Panel*, was the most comprehensive of the RAND American Youth Panels that were conducted to learn how and why youth are using AI for school-related purposes.

In this study, conducted in December 2025, RAND shared its five key findings; of most relevance and interest for the purposes of this book was that "67 percent of students endorsed the statement 'The more students use AI for their schoolwork, the more it will harm their critical thinking skills,' a number up more than 10 percentage points from ten months earlier." The other key findings were:

- The share of students in middle school grades and up who reported using AI for help with their homework increased from 48% in May 2025 to 62% in December 2025. Use among middle and high schoolers drove the overall increase.
- With the exception of using AI to get answers for homework, most students did not feel that their use of AI for other school-related purposes constituted cheating.

- Students in higher grade levels were more likely than students in lower grade levels to (1) say that their schools' rules for AI use depended on the specific teacher, (2) believe that their teachers were checking students' homework for AI use, and (3) worry about being accused of using AI to cheat.
- More female than male students believed that AI use harms their critical thinking skills, and thought that their teachers were checking homework for AI use.

Finally, in January 2026, the **OECD** published its *Digital Education Outlook 2026: Exploring Effective Uses of Generative AI in Education.* Its mission was to synthesize "evidence and expert insights to show how generative AI has the potential to transform the quality and effectiveness of learning, as well as the productivity of education systems, provided its associated risks are carefully managed" (OECD, 2026).

It is worth delving deeper into other educational organizational initiatives that have been addressing AI in the classroom. To that end, I spoke with two leaders: Kari Kivinen, an education outreach expert at the European Union Intellectual Property Office (EUIPO) and a former Secretary-General of the European School system, and Michael Johnston, a cognitive scientist and Senior Fellow at The New Zealand Initiative, where he leads its work on education, and is co-author of *The Memory Paradox* (Oakley et al., 2025).

In our discussion, Kivinen talked about his concern that AI is making everyone a bit lazy, because it produces professional-looking answers that "are often total nonsense, completely stripping away the sources we need to check for credibility." And that since even search engines like Google are adding AI summaries, students are "happily settling for the very first response they see, which is doing some real damage to deep learning."

To describe his concerns, Kivinen employs a standard but appropriate gym metaphor: that is, if you want to build muscle mass, you can't outsource the lifting—you have to do the heavy work yourself to get the benefits. But he also notes that it is really an uphill battle since tech platforms pour billions into hiring the best psychologists just to hook kids' attention.

But Kivinen is not doe banning AI; instead, he believes in leaning into education and a culture of transparency and believes in the idea of "Hybrid Intelligence," where humans and AI play to their unique strengths to work together responsibly. He also makes a very important point: this isn't *only* a student problem, and we have to help adults step up too, which is why his team is going to town halls and public libraries to make sure everyone learns to use AI to promote learning rather than completely replacing it.

Michael Johnston has said that he is seriously worried about cognitive offloading and argues that if we treat technology as a substitute for learning, we are essentially making ourselves intellectually weaker. He refines this point by saying that if we rely on technology as a substitute for learning, we become less intellectually powerful in the long run. He compares it to learning arithmetic: if a child uses a calculator before learning to add, they never learn the skill. Similarly, although some educators are permitting AI for brainstorming purposes, Johnston does not like the idea, especially for younger students, because he wants them to get used to generating ideas for themselves. For 16-to-20-year-olds, though, he added, there is probably less harm, but he still prefers they interact organically with one another to form relationships.

Looking at the bigger picture, Johnston said his deepest anxieties revolve around the social risks of young people forming emotional attachments to bots, which he describes as a seductive and unhealthy illusion. He urges educators to keep young children away from technology as much as possible so they can build rich, independent mental models of the world before they ever touch an AI.

Works Cited

Berkman, R. (2025). The impact of AI on critical thinking: What is the research telling us? *The Information Advisor's Guide to Internet Research, 37*(5).

Burns, M., Winthrop, R., Luther, N., Venetis, E., & Karim, R. (2026, January). *A new direction for students in an AI world: Prosper, prepare, protect.* Center for Universal Education at The Brookings Institution.

The College Board. (2026, February 25). *How educators view AI* [Research brief].

Fu, Y., et al. (2026). *Everyone's using it but no one is allowed to talk about it: College students' experiences navigating the higher education environment in a generative AI world* (arXiv:2602.17720).

Gerlich, M. (2025). AI tools in society: Impacts on cognitive offloading and the future of critical thinking. *Societies, 15*(1), 6.

Harris, T., & Barcay, D. (Hosts). (2025, April 21). Rethinking school in the age of AI (No. 108) [Audio podcast episode]. In *Your undivided attention.* Center for Humane Technology.

Kosmyna, N. (2026). *Your brain on ChatGPT: Accumulation of cognitive debt when using an AI assistant for essay writing task* [Research report]. MIT Media Lab.

OECD. (2026). *OECD Digital Education Outlook 2026: Exploring effective uses of generative AI in education.* OECD Publishing.

Pew Research Center. (2025, December). *Teens, social media and AI chatbots 2025.* 12/PI_2025.12.09_Teens-Social-Media-AI_REPORT.pdf

Schwartz, H. L., Doss, C. J., & Yuan, T. (2025). *More students use AI for homework, and more believe it harms critical thinking: Selected findings from the American Youth Panel* (Research Report No. RRA4742-1). RAND Corporation.

Timmis, K., et.al. (2025). Scientists' warning to humanity: The need to begin teaching critical and systems thinking early in life. *Microbial Biotechnology, 18*(12), e70270.

Turnitin, & Vanson Bourne. (2025, April). *Crossroads: Navigating the intersection of AI in education.* Turnitin.

2 Voices from the Field: Part 1

Creating AI-Resilient Assignments

The following educators all designed courses to minimize the use of AI, either through their pedagogy, assignment design, methods for assessment, or other strategies.

Dr. George Cusack, Director of Academic AI Initiatives, Director of Writing Across the Curriculum, and a Senior Lecturer in English at Carleton College, Northfield, MN

We had a comfortable illusion in academia for years that a polished product equals learning. We figured students' short-circuiting that process were a minority. Now that we have technology that can simulate intellectual work, we have to actually look at what our students are doing as they are doing it.

Dr. Cusack, who helps faculty at his university with writing instruction for his students, argues that the most effective strategies for creating AI-resistant assignments are to follow timeless best practices in writing instruction that focus on the learning process rather than a polished final product and shares it below.

RB: What is the main goal of the Writing Across the Curriculum Program?

GC: It's primarily faculty development around writing. This includes workshops, consulting with individual faculty on assignment design, and institutional assessment of writing. Carleton has a writing portfolio program that every sophomore has to go through, and I oversee that.

RB: What was the theme of the article you wrote on your website, titled "AI-Resistant Assignments"?

GC: It turns out that the strategies for making AI-resistant assignments are also just best practices in writing assignment design. AI changes a lot ,but those strategies are pretty evergreen.

RB: What do you think primarily prevents teachers from using these best practices more frequently?

GC: A big part of it is time. Anytime you go beyond "produce this product and I'll grade it when it's done," you are, by definition, adding time and

DOI: 10.4324/9781003770978-3

work to instructors. At a teaching-focused school like Carleton, our class sizes and student-teacher ratios are small, so I feel like there isn't a lot of excuse. However, when you get to bigger schools with higher teaching loads, it gets to be a lot.

The other part is that outside of folks in writing studies or English scholars from programs with robust writing components, most college faculty are not taught how to teach writing.

So, there's a perception, to some degree, that it's someone else's job.

RB: So, I can assume that writing professors are likely integrating a fair amount of what you advise, and your audience is actually professors *not* trained in writing who want to help their students write well?

GC: That's accurate. My explicit job is WAC coordinator, but as someone who's been doing this for 30 years, the idea that writing instruction can be confined to one corner of the curriculum and naturally transfer to other classes is a fairy tale. If chemists want their students to write like chemists, then the chemists have to teach them to do so. The focus of my faculty development is teaching other faculty how to bring practices refined in writing studies into their own classes.

RB: What sort of reactions have you been getting from those faculty when you show them these skills?

GC: Mostly positive. Again, Carleton already had writing across the disciplines woven into its DNA. It wasn't a hard sell to get faculty to look structurally at their assignments regarding AI. It was mostly about reminding them that the best practices they've heard of for years also apply to AI.

RB: In an ideal world, would you like what you're teaching in this article to be considered by all college professors, no matter what they are teaching?

GC: Yes, absolutely. These design elements are about making the process of the assignment transparent to students and building in places where the instructor can see the student working and intervene. That would be beneficial even if ChatGPT had never come into our lives. I've changed very little about that article in three years because it's really about making an assignment a learning experience rather than just a product.

We had a comfortable illusion in academia for years that a polished product equals learning. We figured students short-circuiting that process were a minority. Now that we have technology that can simulate intellectual work, we have to actually look at what our students are doing as they are doing it.

RB: It sounds like these concepts of scaffolding and reflection could be used by professors in other subjects to show that students are learning the subject matter, not just the writing.

GC: Exactly. There are practices that improve the quality of the assignment for students.

RB: Regarding motivation, what motivates an institution to provide the structure (workshops, training, time), and what motivates teachers to actually do it when they are swamped?

GC: Institutionally, it's about providing resources, primarily time. What is the student-teacher ratio? Do they have the capacity to work with students in-process? A robust faculty development program that is responsive to what faculty are struggling with is essential.

Beyond that, you need an institutional culture that doesn't just say it values teaching, but values a *conversation* around teaching—the idea that teaching is something we are constantly working on and exchanging ideas about.

RB: What could motivate an institution to do this if they don't already?

GC: Having worked at various institutions—from the University of Oklahoma to community-serving universities—my experience is that if you don't incentivize teaching as part of promotion and expected job duties, you give faculty no incentive to get better. If you don't recognize efforts in tenure packets or reviews, you aren't defining teaching as part of their job for all intents and purposes.

RB: What do you think of the concept of "Socratic AI" bots designed to answer questions and prompt students?

GC: It's interesting. I'm currently teaching a class called "Writing with AI." For our last exercise, I had students create bots. I had the idea to create a "reflection bot" instead of a regular writing assignment. It was awful.

What that told me is that while interactive AI tools can be beneficial—like a colleague in physics who built a tool for practice questions—they have limits. She told her students it wasn't always accurate and to treat it like a peer rather than a "sage." That worked. But reflection on one's own writing requires human connection. If students don't believe you are reading it, it becomes soul-killingly perfunctory. The AI sounded sycophantic. Even if it were better, they know it's just an algorithm programmed to sound like it cares.

RB: People say these bots "scale" for large classes where you can't have individual conversations. What is your response to that?

GC: I fully respect that many faculty don't have my student-teacher ratio and have to cut corners. But we must understand that when we depersonalize education by removing people, students feel that. It might be worth providing a tool that gives a version of that conversation at scale, but it would be a heck of a lot better to put more people into that class. If you have 100 students and no TAs, you are disadvantaging them in a way that AI only partially fixes.

There are ways to build around it. If I had 50 students doing a weekly reading response scored by a robot, I'd want the tool to bring forward random responses so I can see what they are saying, score a few myself, and mention them in lectures.

RB: Is there anything else about engaging students in learning that deserves more attention?

GC: I talk about metacognition—students' understanding of their own learning. This needs to be part of AI literacy. Students need to understand that technology isn't really thinking. Every AI guide tells students to "monitor their own learning," but no one tells them what that means. We don't know the best practices yet.

Instructors need to have transparent discussions: "Here is what I designed this assignment to teach you; here is how you know if you are actually doing the work." We have to treat students with respect. The more we police them, the more adversarial the relationship becomes, and the more they look for ways to get around it.

RB: Are you pulling in librarians for AI literacy?

GC: Yes. Librarians are on the front lines regarding how AI affects research. If you have students do research, the relationship with your librarian is the most important teaching partnership you have. They see how students are thinking differently about sources.

RB: This book's premise is that young people are building critical thinking skills through "productive struggle," and that offloading this to AI degrades those neural connections. Do you feel this is a real concern?

GC: Yes. Many things in the world children grow up in now short-circuit critical thinking; AI is just one piece. When you ask students what learning looks like, they still say it is hard, takes time, and involves work. We are all born with the ability to feel bored. Boredom is feeling under-challenged or under-stimulated. Technology can provide immediate gratification for boredom, but the drive for challenge remains.

RB: What is your take on EdTech companies? Are they part of the problem or the solution?

GC: We have become far too reliant on EdTech. I feel like the AI age is accelerating the use of EdTech to "band-aid" over structural problems in our educational system. *Teaching Machines* by Audrey Waters is revelatory on this—the pursuit of technology to solve the problem of needing more teachers goes back to the 19th century.

EdTech has become a big business. We went from "Should we give tablets?" to "If your school can't give everyone a tablet, it's behind." It appeals to instructors because it cuts costs and grading time, but we hand over the autonomy of individual teachers to these platforms.

Regarding AI specifically, companies like Grammarly market "agentic" features directly to students, claiming they will turn writing from hours into minutes without undermining learning. At the same time, they tell schools they can control what students do. They are trying to turn students into lifelong consumers. Student learning is not really in their financial interest; it's about making students customers for life.

RB: Do people raise eyebrows when they see a class called "Writing with AI"?

GC: Absolutely. People generally trust me here, but it definitely raised eyebrows in the English department. There is a concern that I'm just teaching students to cheat better. But the first sentence in the course description is: "Is writing with AI a contradiction in terms?" I frame it as an inquiry. For several projects, my students' conclusion was that it was "bullshit"—they didn't learn or do anything, and they should have just written it themselves. Students don't want to lose their own voice. As one teacher said, "I don't want to grade the AI's work; I want to know what you think."

George Cusack is the Director of Academic AI Initiatives, Director of Writing Across the Curriculum, and a Senior Lecturer in English at Carleton College. He received his PhD in English with a specialty in Irish Drama from the University of Oregon, but for the 30 years since, he's primarily taught writing and worked in faculty development around writing and instructional design. He's the co-editor of the forthcoming scholarly anthology Artificial Intelligence in Writing Program Administration (Parlor Press, 2007).

Dr. Kyle D. S. Maclean, Assistant Professor and Teaching Scholar at Western University's Ivey Business School, London, ON

Students can use AI but they'll have to use it to explain it to them so they understand it. Because I will be asking THEM the questions, not AI.

To ensure academic integrity against AI manipulation, Dr. Maclean, who teaches both without and with AI, implements live, interactive presentations with spontaneous question-and-answer sessions, and since his business course is about how a consultant can present findings with clients, he frames these as client consultations. He has also created an "AI Intern" chatbot built on GPT-5 to create gamified business case studies, forcing students to decide what data to extract while tracking their conversational logs to evaluate their real-time strategic thinking.

RB: So, from what I understand, in 2021 you designed your course, Decision Making with Analytics so that the students would need to do an oral exam at the end of the semester. Is that correct?

KM: Yes, in 2020, during COVID, we tried something we called a "scalable oral exam." We were concerned about academic integrity as everything moved online. We sent students a question and gave them five minutes to respond with a video answer. In effect, it was a simultaneous oral exam for everyone.

RB: So how did it go?

KM: It went well. We could very quickly tell who knew what they were talking about. That said, students didn't like it—and that aligns with the research. Oral exams are stressful. They require students to think on their feet, without rehearsing answers. And when it's live, they're speaking directly to a faculty member they respect, which adds pressure.

But I did not call it an oral exam. I'm calling it a presentation with questions and answers, the key, though, is we did it live and in person (the one in Fall of 2020 was done by students recording videos within a certain limited period of time).

RB: Was the primary purpose of designing the assignment this way to ensure academic integrity was maintained in an all-online teaching environment?

KM: It was designed to serve several purposes. In this particular class we want to teach students how to present ideas and communicate them to a client, so it serves that purpose, and they know I am going to ask questions as well, just as a client would.

So, what they are preparing for as a consultation is that they gather a lot of background information, they make an analysis, and then they present their findings to a client.

RB: So, this mode of doing an online presentation live is also something that could be used to create a more AI-resilient assignment as well, correct?

KM: Yes. Students can use AI, but they'll have to use it to explain it to them so they understand it. Because I will be asking THEM the questions, not AI.

RB: Your assignment could not prevent anyone from using AI in an unauthorized way before the oral exam, though, right?

KM: Sure, if anyone wants to cheat, they still can, but they will need to do it with effort, so this puts up some barriers. It makes it harder like locks on a door.

RB: What are the downsides or drawbacks of an in-person oral exam?

KM: Primarily scalability. We are testing their higher-order skills, which, unlike say multiple choice, requires more faculty effort to assess. But say the class was 150 students, an oral exam would be very hard to do. So, I do it by creating groups. For our 2021 assignment, we released a question and the student had to do a video and send it in right away.

But in this newer Sports/Entertainment Analytics class, which we did in 2025, we had 75 people and grouped them into teams of four. There were slots during the day in the classroom where they could make their presentation.

RB: Other than the matter of scalability, what other factors represent hurdles or challenges in setting up an assignment like this?

KM: Well it is clear that students get very stressed about it, especially when it is individual and called an "oral exam." That was why I called it a presentation with Q&A. Other hurdles include how to consistently grade, especially when a conversation goes in various directions. There is also a risk in a team oral presentation that one person did all the work and answers the questions. So, to avoid this, I prewarn the teams that I may point to any student at any time to ask them a question.

RB: And to clarify, for this assignment students are permitted to use AI on their own for background research?

KM: Yes, they can do their research via an LLM—as this is a replication of what a consultant might do—gather information, make an analysis, and present it to a client. If they use AI to explain it to them, fine, but when they are in front of the client and talking about it and answering questions, they need to have put it to memory and re-explain things. It's a start and not a replacement for the learning process: using AI to help you understand a problem is not of concern. Now, if they just take all of my questions and plug it in and get the answer, that might be a problem.

Students are also assessed with a closed-book exam in the classroom. They have their laptop, but there is no Internet and no access to their files either. The reason we don't allow them to access their files is that some students may have local versions of an AI product that they can run without being online. To enable this, we use a software called ExamSoft.

RB: What else would you advise someone else who wants to try real-time oral exams as you did?

KM: One is to record the sessions so you don't need to grade in the moment. I might jot down some things initially and look at the recording later. I don't want to be rushed. Grading later from recordings also helps avoid the "sequencing effect" which can happen from grading as you go, making grading inconsistent.

Also to save time and avoid the slowdown of technical glitches during presentation, have them send to you their materials the night before. Also, give them a grading rubric.

Finally, you might have to address an accommodation request from a student who has anxiety or fear of speaking in front of a group. Here I'd say that faculty should remember that these need to be *reasonable* accommodations; an accommodation that subverts the goal of the class would not be reasonable. One way around this is just to give everybody in the class a longer amount of time than you might have normally, and that avoids process variation.

RB: Are there ways in which you are integrating AI as a means for *eliciting* critical thinking?

KM: Yes, we also teach via case methods, where students read a case and then make a recommendation to a fictional client. The challenge with academic cases is that the students get all the information at once and then make a recommendation. But in the real world, you get a little bit of information, then you go out in the world, test your hypothesis, check it, explore, and so on. So how do we replicate the dynamic case experience in the classroom? Here we developed an AI Intern to help students.

RB: Tell me more about how it works.

KM: The way it works is that the AI provides a simulated conversation. The case we created is called the HopeWorks Foundation, a non-profit, and the students need to figure out: How do we increase donations to this organization?

We've gamified it in a way so that when a student asks for certain data in the AI chatbot we built, they actually get new data that has been trained on about this fictional foundation. It's up to the student to think to ask for what they need to get it. So when you ask for, oh, do we have donations in dollars per visit? And the answer may be, yes, I got that. And another question, for example, could be do you have data on the foundation's social media followers?

And when they click it, they can run a regression on the data that they have, for instance, or they can see a line chart of donations over time. But they only get the data if they ask for it.

Another feature it offers is that if I click on the name of a student, I can see the conversation the student actually had with the AI. So, in class I could say, okay, like, walk me through your thought process of why you thought to ask for this information.

I can actually walk through the students' thought process. I may say, tell me about your internal theory at that point, and why did you think this information you ask for might be helpful? So, I am very bullish slash excited about having students be able to ask for more information. I think that's absolutely going to change how we teach business cases.

RB: How can this model be applied for other courses or applications in business schools?

KM: So you can imagine it working in operations, where instead of just talking to one person, when you're talking to the AI intern, you can have communications to or from various staff, perhaps the CEO, the COO, or the floor supervisor of the factory. And maybe all of those people have slightly different pieces of information about what's going on.

RB: What is the foundation of this model you built? How does it access the knowledge it needs to respond to the questions?

KM: The web development work I did was built on GPT-5, so it not only has information for this case study, but also has its larger world knowledge, which it needs. However, by using the API and creating prompts we have finer control. The system instructions take precedence over the user prompts. The way the programming works is that we tell the LLM that you're going to get certain messages from people and basically, here's how you respond. That system message has all the background information that we want them to declare. The key with prompting is the system message in the developer instructions. I built it with software called Replit.

The other thing I did was build an AI agent that goes out every day and finds a piece of news that relates to our course—and then it says, oh you are using optimization, and here it is relevant to our course.

Right now, I'm trying to build a platform where anyone can do this in their own course.

Dr. Kyle D. S. Maclean is an Assistant Professor and Teaching Scholar at Western University's Ivey Business School (London, ON), where he teaches business analytics, management science, and operations research. His research focuses on revenue management in live entertainment and scalable teaching tools for undergraduate classrooms.

Laura Morrison, EdD, Assistant Professor, Frazer Faculty of Education,

Ontario Tech University, Oshawa, ON

AI can be a writing partner, but it's a slippery slope—it can augment the writing but it can also unintentionally slip into a murky area where it is doing synthesis, analysis or even reasoning.

To foster critical AI literacy, Morrison has structured her writing assignments as an iterative, multi-step process where students must first submit a completely unassisted piece of writing to establish their baseline voice and reveal specific areas needing structural improvement. Next, students execute a "creative remix" of their original text using generative AI to refine style and mechanics, followed by an instructor-evaluated comparison template analyzing how the tool altered their personal voice, accuracy, and human agency. Finally, she leverages a mandatory reflective cover page for all coursework to evaluate how students integrated prior feedback and utilized AI.

RB: Laura, please let me know what you have been doing as it relates to AI and learning.

LM: I teach an undergraduate course in writing and information literacy. The biggest impact that AI has had on the course was when LLMs hit the market in November 2022 when I taught it again. At that time, I embedded some critical AI into the process, but we did not yet have a policy on how it should be used.

But more recently, I taught the same course again in 2025 and this time did it completely differently and it integrated critical AI literacy where I taught students the reflective skills they needed so that they are aware and using it intentionally and critically. I also completely redesigned the assignments: for example, in the AI and Authorship assignment I have them write something completely unsupported by AI; then they rewrite it using GenAI with some help with matters like style and organization. And then there is a reflection portion where they compare and contrast the versions.

RB: Tell me more about that reflection portion.

LM: They examine matters like how their voice was impacted, the accuracy, and more. I gave them a template to use to do this, which was my attempt to recognize the way AI has impacted their work, again allowing them to use it but then reflect on the outcome. I wanted them to think whether AI made their writing more vague or general and was it still true to your own experience.

I also asked them to examine how it tweaked certain things too. That was a good way to get them to think critically. And for all assignments they needed to create a cover page where they had to reflect how their assignment matched the assessment criteria, and because the assignment was an iterative process how previous feedback was integrated- and how Gen AI was used.

RB: What kind of feedback did you get from the students on the use and impact of AI on their writing?

LM: There was quite a range of views. Some said they never used it or only minimally and some of them said they would never use it again because they don't like how it manipulated their voice. Others said yes, it was helpful for strengthening sentence structure and writing mechanics like that. Others had more awareness of matters related to change of voice and ownership.

RB: Do you try to detect or look for any unauthorized AI usage? Is there a way to check?

LM: It's hard to say, I really don't know how the students honestly used AI in that assignment.

But I am transparent that I use the AI Detector GPT 0 for an initial check, but really only for papers where I suspect it was used. Then, if the software says yes, it was 100% from AI, I reach out to the student to talk about how they used it. Half the time they tell me, and acknowledge it, and often they say yes, I was rushed; others have gotten better at hiding they are using it or stopped using it.

RB: Some faculty are acknowledging that with proper and restricted use, AI can be seen as a kind of collaborator or partner. How do you feel about that?

LM: I am thinking more that AI can be a writing partner, but it's a slippery slope. It can augment the writing, but it can also unintentionally slip into a murky area where it is doing synthesis, analysis, or even reasoning. So when we're using ChatGPT is it doing heavy lifting?

I do see some specific values though. For example, students with ADHD have a million thoughts at one time. If they can use ChatGPT to help them elaborate or connect ideas, it can be used as an assistive technology that could really help. So, it may help them with critical thinking.

RB: What are just a few of the most important lessons learned and advice you would give to other educators who want to do the same as you did? Any special dos or don'ts?

LM: I just want to preface this by saying: Nothing is a hard-and-fast "Do" or "Don't". Everything is context…Having said that…

Do: Frame the assignment so they don't begin with AI and use their own abilities to do their own writing.

Do: Lay foundations of critical digital literacies and critical AI literacies.

Do: Include resources on how to use GenAI for those who have never used it before.

Do: Have the original piece of writing due first, then the creative remix and then both together with the critical reflection on the changes made by AI, the implications for voice, bias, accuracy, ethics, human agency and cognition, the student's personal stance on AI in the writing process, and how this shapes their understanding of authorship and creativity in digital contexts.

Don't: Have them submit everything at once. Provide instructor and/or peer feedback for each of the three components (the original writing, the remix, the critical reflection) so as to mimic the iterative writing process.

Don't: Allow them to use GenAI (even Grammarly) for the original, in order to uncover the students' specific needs in terms of writing improvement (i.e., grammar, spelling, thought organization, overall structural organization) if one of the goals of the assignment is to actually improve the students' core writing abilities. However, it's possible we are in a post-writing age where developing these skills is no longer necessary…it's ALL context-based (dependent on the institution, the course, the professor, etc.). Also, if students need certain AI tools because of accommodation (i.e., ELLs, students with communication challenges, Autism, ADHD, etc. that changes things, too…) Nothing is a hard-and-fast "Do" or "Don't". Everything is context.

RB: Is there anything important we did not talk about?

LM: We need to teach critical AI literacy skills alongside metacognitive thinking, and future assignments could be structured to minimize AI use initially to better assess students' abilities.

I believe collectively we have to decide as a human race where we want to draw the line for our dependence on technology and our offloading to AI. Do we give in and understand that historically we've offloaded or do we take a different perspective?

Dr. Laura Morrison is an Assistant Professor in the Learning Sciences at Ontario Tech University, where her research explores critical AI literacy and innovative, technology-supported approaches to teaching and learning. She leads collaborative, community-engaged projects, including the co-development of a culture-based AI learning agent designed to support equitable STEM engagement.

Laura.Morrison@ontariotechu.ca

**Lauren Himbeault, Instructor, Computer Science,
University of Manitoba, Winnipeg**

We're not giving students the chance to strengthen the muscle, to learn, actually, how to be a person with integrity. They're not learning that, they're too scared, so they just sit there and do nothing, or they cheat and get in trouble. There's no slowly adding that weight when you're training up to the big day.

Lauren Himbeault wants to foster authentic learning, and she does so by implementing structured AI prompt journals and "sources.txt" files, in order to formalize a reflective process that acts as a cognitive forcing function to track exactly how students engage with digital tools. She also cultivates a highly transparent and approachable classroom environment by modeling her own problem-solving process, including mistakes and prompt-driven development—while pairing these expectations with flexible deadlines to dramatically reduce deadline-driven panic cheating.

RB: Tell me how your form of assessment and teaching differs from standard methods.

LH: First, with every assignment they submitted they had to submit the names of their sources—so as long as they submitted sources there would be no academic integrity issues—you just need to tell me what you used, including AI through the use of prompt journals.

Source citation was required in all courses I taught prior to generative AI (since approximately 2019). Structured AI prompt journals were introduced for the first time this Winter 2026 (post-GenAI) to encourage reflective use and better understand how students were engaging with these tools. Informal reflection and emphasis on problem-solving existed before generative AI, but the prompt journals later formalized and deepened this reflective component.

Having them reflect has them use their brain in ways that AI cannot. This forces them to reflect in a meaningful way and helps avoid academic integrity issues.

That's where it started and it worked well. One reason was that students trusted me enough so that they would come to me and say that they tried the easy way out [and relied on AI]-that was a huge step forward- and they wanted to do better.

RB: What did you do to create this trusted environment?

LH: For one thing, I am quite transparent in my teachings, including the use of AI. I'll say, so let's address the elephant in the room. Here is how I use it to solve problems but not replace my thinking. I show them how I solve problems, not replace my thinking. I show students that I may use it, and they can see that I will make mistakes in class solving a problem and students like that. I'm slowly using the term prompt-driven development. Using prompts to gain a better understanding and move forward, as opposed to replacing my brain.

This also makes me more approachable. And I tell them that my job is not to have you not cheat—at the end of the day you are your own person—if you are not, eventually it will catch up to you. There's no way around that, so I want to give you opportunities to use your brain first.

RB: What other changes did you make in the assignment?

LH: Flexible deadlines were introduced later alongside auto-grading to support accessibility and reduce administrative overhead. While not originally AI-driven, they appeared to reduce deadline-related stress and impulsive decisions such as outsourcing work or over-reliance on AI.

One other advantage is that this appeared to reduce the number of late-night complaints and panicked emails I received.

RB: What spurred you to begin your initiative in rethinking assessment

LH: I've taught in a variety of venues, both academic and non-academic since I was 18. And I realized teaching is about problem-solving, and my graduate work was in the psychology of learning and computer science education more specifically. I've seen students struggle with questions of academic integrity even before generative AI.

About three years ago, when we got ChatGPT, things started getting intense. I've noticed they have been afraid and not sure how to use it without cheating and getting in trouble. I wanted to help them find the balance of when it is OK and not OK to use it, because often when in school its use is not permitted, but it may be fine in the business world.

Around 2019, I began requiring a sources.txt file with coding assignments. By 2023, I became more explicit with students about why these documents were required and how they were used. In 2025, I introduced flexible deadline adjustments, and in 2026 I added explicit journaling as a cognitive forcing function to support reflective practice.

RB: What was your hoped-for goal here?

LH: To have students in my own field understand the limitations of these tools and their benefits and get them interested enough so they can share what they discovered and disseminate what they learned to others.

RB: What resources did you rely on to create this?

LH: I attended seminars and workshops on people doing neat stuff with GenAI. I was also friends with a colleague in the Psychology department who works in digital literacy and children with digital literacy, who had redesigned her assignments to work with AI.

RB: What were the main barriers or objections you faced along the way to developing this?

LH: Well, I had no funding. So, for example, I paid my friend who helped me with it with ice cream and hugs! But the biggest hurdle is time. I'd like to now do research so I can get more than just anecdotal results but real data.

RB: When you started this, what kind of reactions did you get from others?

LH: I wouldn't say anybody's been negative, or pushed back, or told me not to try and do something using it. But I would say maybe there's been some hesitancy around just how much I am trying to integrate AI into the class.

RB: Is there anything you tried and discovered did not work and you had to modify?

LH: Yes, for one thing, the prompt journals were too long. But the biggest modification I had to make is how do you get students to reflect without it being something that they just won't do? If they are used to cognitive offloading asking them to do something cognitively difficult, like reflect for 25 minutes, won't work. It's exhausting to them. They will give me one-liners. I've seen it happen, many times, so I'm trying to strike a balance between getting them to see how meaningful it is to do this and making it not so burdensome.

Students will even say, "now I'm procrastinating on my reflection!". So, I often talk about how integrity is like muscle. You know, if you go to the gym to go work out your trainer doesn't say don't work out for three weeks, because you have a big tournament coming up. They say we're going to slowly keep adding weights until we get there. And that's kind of how I feel about building academic integrity. It's problem-solving and we need to get there slowly, start building that muscle early, by integrating these conversations early, and then by the time they reach a place where they really need to use it, you can push them out of the nest, and they'll be able to flex that muscle, and have strengthened it enough that they can use it.

We're not giving students the chance to strengthen the muscle, to learn, actually, how to be a person with integrity. They're not learning that, they're too scared, so they just sit there and do nothing, or they cheat and get in trouble. There's no slowly adding that weight when you're training up to the big day.

RB: What are a few of the most important lessons you've learned and advice you would offer to other educators who want to do the same thing you did?

LH: The first one, the biggest one is the need for being transparent with your students. We can't pretend like we don't know what AI is, or that we're not going to use it. So, honesty and transparency makes you somebody that your students will actually want to talk to about this with.

Second, remember that school is about the learning journey and education not about being punitive. You need to cultivate an atmosphere that we are in an environment where we all make mistakes.

And you do have to use AI yourself. True learning requires discomfort, and if you are too nervous and hesitant about using it, how can you help the students if you have not done this yourself?

RB: One question that I like to ask everyone I interview is what, if anything, do you think could motivate a student on their own, through their own free choice, to decide not to turn to AI when it is not appropriate or good for them in some way to do so.

LH: I think, like anything, there's a normal distribution of students on that spectrum. So, we've got students who will be self-motivated. I have one student who regularly tells me that a healthy dose of fear helps her make sure she doesn't cheat. So, I love that for… she's like, it's very motivating!

And there are students in the middle, and there are students that you can say everything to, and they're still going to do their best to try to pull the wool over your eyes.

Self-motivation is really tricky. Evolutionarily our brains are happy to take shortcuts as we have a million and one things we have to do. We can explain the psychology of that and why we have to interrupt it when you are learning to learn. But institutions are so punitive.

RB: So What's Next?

LH: I did not collect any quantitative data on how my previous classes worked, so this term I will be doing that. It's still preliminary but in my third-year software engineering class of 160 students I am doing something new and collecting data.

These projects emphasize system-level design quality (e.g., cohesion, coupling, maintainability) in addition to functionality. Large-scale AI-generated solutions typically produce poorly structured code that does not meet course design standards, making wholesale outsourcing to AI incredibly ineffective but I told them they can use AI if they want as long as they are using AI prompt journals. I told them they can use AI as they want—I just want the data from the journals—did you use it and if so how did you just copy code, have conversations, etc.

Lauren Himbeault is a Computer Science instructor at the University of Manitoba. Her teaching focuses on problem-solving, transparent assessment, and supporting ethical, reflective use of generative AI in computing education.

Contact: lauren.himbeault@umanitoba.ca or www.laurenhimbeault.com

---

Dr. Matthew Fledderjohann, Director, Writing Center at Le Moyne College, Syracuse, NY

> *If you use it and don't tell me, well, the only thing you have to lose is your sense of integrity, right? Yes, you could lie to me, and I would be none the wiser, but again, is that really the person you want to be? Because if it is the person you want to be, I can't help you within the space of two and a half hours for 15 weeks.*

Dr. Fledderjohann will let his students use generative AI for any purpose—as long as they maintain complete honesty, tracking their intentions and actual usage through formal reflection check-ins at the beginning, middle, and end of the semester. He pairs this transparency with contract grading, allowing students to earn marks above a baseline "B" by writing an optional, human-only reflection essay examining the cognitive benefits and psychological challenges of intentionally stepping away from AI. His focus, which aligns with the Jesuit University he teaches at, is *Cura Personalis*-Care of the Whole Person.

RB: Your goal, if I understand this correctly, has been to try to help students make ethical and appropriate choices when using AI. And you did this in your Fall 2025 senior-level capstone course on death and dying at Le Moyne College. There you helped students, as you put it, think deeply about why they are here, to be accountable to themselves, and how they want to engage in the learning process.

My first question is what spurred you to begin this initiative?

MF: So, I've been engaging closely with AI since November 2022. I am a compositionist and study writing and how we teach it. Even back when I started then I knew AI would be interesting in the writing sphere and impact how we teach the writing process and will force us to teach it in a different way.

RB: Tell me a little about your background.

MF: Here at Le Moyne, I'm the Writing Center Director, and I also direct our Center for Teaching and Learning. And so, I was working with faculty to talk through with them about how they're responding to generative AI. A lot of the early talk was about, well, how can we remediate assignments to make them, you know, generative AI proof?

But as AI has become more and more powerful, that's become less and less of a viable option. And so, this past semester, I took a turn toward radical transparency so that in front of my students I could say, like, look, guys, I think I've developed some meaningful assignments for you all, some assignments that are going to help you engage with this content that matters in a valuable way.

And the reality of it is, you could turn to generative AI, and you could probably get a B in the class as it can do that level of work, and you could probably get away with it.

But what kind of person do you want to be?

So even before I started, my new policy was to tell students, OK just use AI in whatever ways you want, in whatever ways you think are most beneficial to you, but just let me know.

And I'm going to ask you to be accountable for your decisions. I want you to, at the beginning of the semester, use a form to tell me what your intentions are about generative AI use. We had another form at the midpoint of the semester to say, okay, this is what you said, you were going to use generative AI on some of your assignments, you know, I ask you to tell me, and you haven't told me that you've used generative AI, so I assume you haven't. So, have you? And then there was another check-in at the end of the semester to say, hey, did you use generative AI?

And since there was no punishment I told them they could use it; I just wanted them to let me know. And I told them if you use it and don't tell me, well, the only thing you have to lose is your sense of integrity, right? Yes, you could lie to me, and I would be none the wiser, but again, is that really the person you want to be? Because if it is the person you want to be I can't help you within the space of two and a half hours for 15 weeks, right? I can't change your sense of moral integrity, but I at least can, I don't know, make you feel bad if you're lying about it.

RB: What are some of the big questions you posed to them?

MF: So, I start it all off by asking them really specifically, why are you here? You know, it's 11:15 am on January 28th and you're sitting in this classroom, why?

And then they write their answer to that. And then my next question is, you enrolled in this class. Why did you enroll in this class? And then, why are you at this college? Why are you at Le Moyne? And then my final question is why are you here at all, right? Like, why do you exist? You are breathing, and you are thinking, and you are having experiences, and so you are alive! As a human, yeah.

And so, then we talk about is there any connection for you? Is there any through line? So, when you think about how you answer the question about what your purpose is, does that go back to why you're at this college, or why you're in this class, or maybe even why you showed up today?

And then we could have a conversation about what's your purpose. And how do you see that your purpose isn't this thing that exists externally to you that you'll achieve at some other point, but rather it's only ever manifested in the present, right? What are you doing with your life right now?

And I've been telling my students and then other students look, if you're being here right now doesn't have any purpose for you, maybe don't be here, right? So, your life is short, and all this is predicated, too, on the fact that I did this with a class that's about death and dying, where we talk about the fact that we're all going to die, right?

Like, we know where this ends. We know that we have a limited amount of time, and what are we doing with the time that we have?

But regardless of the content, asking students to say, if you don't see any inherent value in what you're doing here, maybe this isn't the right place for you, right? Maybe you need to go find the thing that you do find inherent value in, since your life is short, I would like you to live a good life, and find joy and fulfillment with the things that you're doing and the people that you're connected to.

RB: What was your hoped-for overall goal in the class?

MF: A couple of things. One, to help the students be accountable for their behavior and for their learning. So that at the bare minimum, they were thinking critically about why they were doing what they did and what they were doing within the learning space. So, like, yes, I'm choosing to use generative AI, and I'm choosing it for these reasons.

So, I think that accountability to the student's own learning connects to this other purpose of helping students think about and interact with internal motivation about what is it that's driving me to learn? And then, even more importantly, what is it that's driving me to live? So, to be a person in communication and in community with other people.

RB: Can I assume that being in Jesuit school with a spiritual foundation dimension, you can assume that perhaps, that's one reason why the student chose it, and your approach would be in line with the philosophy of your college?

MF. Sure, it certainly fits into the value of *Cura Personalis*, the idea of the care of the whole person—that's a Jesuit value and I see that as a manifestation of this. And my class was small enough that I could granulate and say what about YOU Frank?—What are the choices YOU are making? And I know who Frank is as a person.

So that small liberal arts approach plus our Jesuit values about caring for personhood matters. And I brought that to the table too with my students. And so, I can also say to them, I want you to also care for *me*.

In the writing assignments I give you, I'm asking you about what you are thinking. And you can use GenAI, but I want to know what *YOU* think—I don't want to know what the computer thinks, or what it says it thinks. But if you are going to use GEN AI to do your thinking and just phone it in and not let me know, I am going to engage with it as if it was YOUR thoughts and that is whom I want to give feedback to. I don't want to give feedback to whatever slop a computer thinks about—I'd rather be playing Lego with my seven-year-old twins. So, consider that I want to engage with your thoughts, and if I can't that will frustrate me.

RB: After the class, did you receive feedback?

MF: I produced a generic Google Doc template that I print out and ask the students to share their academic intentions. As I said, there are three of them, one at the beginning of the semester, one in the middle, and then there's one on the last day of the semester. They gave me feedback about what they were doing, what they intended to do, and then what they actually did.

And so, this served as one mechanism of checking in with them about how things went. And I could see what the students said initially was the extent to which they planned to use generative AI, and then how much they said they actually used it.

It turned out that at the start of the semester, 65% of them said that they were going to use generative AI on some assignments. And only 23% said they were going to use it on none of the assignments. But at the end of the semester, 55% told me that they'd never used generative AI on any of the assignments. These are their own responses, of course, so, you know, we take this with a grain of salt, and we can't prove this. But I can say that I read all of their work, and those numbers made sense to me. There really weren't times where I said this looks like a generative AI thing when a student said they did not use it.

The only qualification here is that a couple of times I noticed some AI-like qualities within some students' writing and they hadn't said they'd used it. So, I approached them and say, "Just so you know, these rhetorical moves you made sound very AI-y. But you didn't say you used AI, so I assume you didn't." And they assured me that they hadn't. So, then we got to have a conversation about why those aspects of their writing looked like AI and how to avoid those moves for future writing and/or for future classes.

RB: Were there other ways you got feedback?

MF: I also do contract grading, in that the contract states that if you do all the work, and it meets the broad clarifications of what you need to do you get a B. If you want to earn a higher grade in my classes, you have to do additional work, or you have to do really, really exemplary work. And one of the ways that they could do additional work was to write a 400-word essay about why they chose not to use generative AI, and what that process was like.

I had seven students take me up on that, and some of the things they said were amazing, including:

> *"I began to synthesize and read what was assigned for my classes on my own again. I was surprised at how bored I got while reading,["having a difficult time applying the necessary thinking skills and paying attention.") or how I was struggling to find words, phrases, or summarize anything without drawing an extreme number of blank thoughts. It was disheartening, but I re-taught myself how to think."*
>
> Another student wrote that "*I would have missed so much by only using ChatGPT for a summary...Because I did everything on my own, I actually had to sit with the readings, films, and conversations in a way I probably would not have done otherwise. Writing without AI meant I had to slow down and figure out what I genuinely believed, instead of relying on something to fill in the thoughts for me. That ended up helping me more than I expected....*
>
> *Even when a topic was uncomfortable, taking the time to put my own voice into every assignment made me reflect instead of shutting down. I could hear myself in everything I turned in, which made the class feel more meaningful."*

Another student talked about how they found themselves talking more with other people outside of the class, with friends and family members about these issues, and being able to do it better because they had done the work themselves.

So, yes, it was seven students out of the class doing this kind of reflection work, but it was certainly validation for me. Even if it's only these seven that were sort of doing this level of reflection as far as I'm concerned, that feels like a win.

And so, it's an attempt to have these heartfelt conversations because, I mean, again how you spend your life matters, and right now, this is how you're spending your life. And so, I've talked to those students about trying to find something that they're interested in. OK, yes, you have to write this paper, and it's about history, and you don't care about it, but, then, what *do* you care about? Do you care about sports? So, would it be of interest to you to think about the history of, say Athenian sports traditions? Or, OK, do you care about fashion? Do you care about, like, inequalities across time? What shows up on your TikTok feed? What are you inherently interested in that the algorithm knows that you like?

How can you leverage that to find the way into this other thing that you have to do anyway? Wouldn't it be more pleasant if you enjoyed it a little bit? Just for your own sake, right? And you will also write better if you're doing something you like.

RB: Is there anything you would do differently in terms of discussion and requirements around AI usage if you were to teach this course again?

MF: Yes. Originally in my syllabus, I was telling students that they can use AI in whatever ways they want, they just had to let me know. But the mechanism that I wanted them to let me know by was a long AI usage acknowledgment. I think one student actually filled out that form. It ended up that students just more informally were saying, oh yeah, I used AI to do this.

So, that form is not going to work. I think moving forward, I'd be requiring students to at the end of every assignment, to just add a line to say either, I didn't use AI for this, or I used X AI bot, for Y purpose, or this one for Z reason, etc. Just one thing is fine, because I still want to have more accountability. I asked for too much, and so I did not get enough accountability. I think trying to find some sort of middle ground with what I can actually ask them to do that doesn't feel like a separate assignment since that wasn't working.

Also, I'd never given reading quizzes before, but I told the students, I value reading, I actually want you to engage with these texts, so we're going to do pop quizzes. And it was just one question—it was specific, but not onerous, as the idea was that if you read the text, you would know the answer to that one question. This was done to build accountability around reading. And I will continue to do that.

RB: Finally, is there anything you would advise other faculty that want to conduct the class in the way you did?

MF: Yes, I would warn them that doing this is time-intensive, not "efficient." But there is value in that, and it takes caring for your students, learning their names, responding to their emails, and a lot of work. And it takes a real sense by the teacher of the value of their work they are doing—you can't BS or fake the value of what you are teaching—*Dr. Fledderjohann directs the writing center and the teaching and learning center at Le Moyne College in Syracuse, NY. With a background in composition and rhetoric and English literature, his teaching and research interests are in writing pedagogy, apocalyptic narratives, and thanatology. His most recent work has been published in Teaching of Psychology, The Peer Review, Praxis, and Enculturation.*

Contact Information: fleddema@lemoyne.edu

Pia Kiikeri is a lecturer at Haaga-Helia Professional Teacher Education College *and at Haaga-Helia University of Applied Sciences, Helsinki, Finland*

Even in a physical classroom, I try to speak very little and let the students do the speaking.

To ensure authentic online evaluation and counter the threat of AI automation, Kiikeri advocates for replacing traditional written essays with student-generated audio and video recordings where learners must speak to articulate their understanding. She utilizes cooperative learning games and "caves and claims" simulations played via Microsoft Teams, requiring small groups to collaboratively solve problems in recorded sessions that teachers later review as the primary assessment of genuine comprehension. A link to her game is provided in the discussion below.

RB: What age or grade level are the students your trainees work with?

PK: They work in vocational education, which is for students around 18–20 years old. In Finland, we call this the "second level" after basic school. But I also train teachers who work in the University of Applied Sciences where students might be 20, 40, or even 50 or 60 years old.

RB: To make these conversations productive, are there specific tips or strategies you give to other teachers?

PK: It is very important that we teachers speak to each other about AI. At Haaga-Helia, my colleagues and I meet once a month for an hour to share what is happening and discuss new programs. For example, things are moving very fast with Google, NotebookLM, and ChatGPT. We use those and Claude as well. We prefer sharing ideas on what programs to use, but we also discuss the pedagogy, what works well and what doesn't.

RB: Have you heard of any specific strategies from those discussions that are working well regarding students and AI?

PK: We think a lot about how we can improve evaluation and assessment. One very good idea I heard from another teacher involves using "plays" or games.

For example, one that I use is where students play a game in a small group. They move through steps or "caves" and take "claims." When they reach a certain point, they open a "card" that has a task that relates to a question. They must speak to each other to solve it, and the meeting is recorded. The teacher then reviews the recording to see what the students are saying and what they have actually understood. That recording serves as the assessment.

RB: And the teacher created this game for the class?

PK: Yes, she created it. The students play it together at home as homework. They use a platform like Microsoft Teams, and it records both video and audio. That way, the teacher can see them and ensure they aren't just going to an AI for the answer.

RB: I like that—it's engaging and fun, which helps with student boredom, and it prevents AI cheating because they are being recorded in live conversation.

PK: Yes, and I have also been working on a game myself. It's on a platform called Puppetry.net. It isn't for assessment, but for learning what AI is. I can show you the Finnish version (see Figure 2.1).

The students move their "car" 1, 2, or 3 spaces. When they land, there is a question card. The group has to speak together to find the answer. If they are online, they go into breakout rooms to do this. Afterward, we have a class discussion about what they learned: What is AI? Why and how should I use it? What happens when I use it?

Figure 2.1 Kiikeri created a digital game that provided methods for students to reflect together about their use of AI.

RB: That's a great idea. Is there anything else important to mention regarding AI and learning?

PK: I also use videos. Many students submit video or audio recordings of themselves speaking instead of just an essay. I listen to those to hear what they have to say. Most of my students are online, so they make these recordings at home, but even in the physical classroom, I try to speak very little and let the students do the speaking.

Finally, I want to see more of this in the curriculum. Currently, the curriculum says very little about AI use. I want it to include more about AI literacy, how to be a smart user, what is good and bad, and how to integrate it into thinking and writing. We need to train students in digital and information literacy as it relates to AI.

[You can try out the game here: bit.ly/4q0C2p3

Pia Kiikeri has 30 years of experience in vocational education and its development. For the past seven years, she has worked as a lecturer at the Haaga-Helia Professional Teacher Education College, developing, among other things, various artificial intelligence and digital pedagogical learning and teaching solutions. She holds a Doctor of Education (KT) degree, is a vocational teacher and a vocational special needs teacher. She trains those who are becoming teachers or are already in training.

Contact: pia.kiikeri@haaga-helia.fi

3 Voices from the Field Part 2

Integrating Educational Focused AI

The following faculty have all taken the tack of integrating AI into their assignments and learning strategies, but with an educational focus.

Vincent Granito, PhD, Professor of Psychology, Lorain County Community College, Elyria, OH

Ultimately, I think AI is less of a tech issue and more of a pedagogy issue. It has forced me to rethink the goals of education... Is giving students a 75-question multiple-choice exam really what we want them to get out of the course?

Dr. Granito turns traditional final exams into dynamic, interactive news-magazine interviews, requiring students to pick a topic, become an expert, and use a specific prompt that commands ChatGPT to rigorously cross-examine them one question at a time, playing the role of a journalist. He says that he was "blown away" by how much ChatGPT really got into its "assignment" of playing a talk show interviewer. To manage writing assignments ethically, he breaks down the research paper into incremental steps, utilizes a flipped classroom to conduct mandatory verbal check-ins with individual students regarding their progress, and explicitly tells his classes that any submission is subject to a verbal review.

RB: What spurred you to begin your project by rethinking assessment in the age of AI?

VG: My background is in psychology, and I am a psychology professor. I also do quite a bit of work with our Teaching and Learning Center, and whenever there is some new technology they come to me and say can you play with it? And they ask me to weigh in.

So shortly after ChatGPT came out in 2022, they approached me and said, "have you ever heard of it?" And I said, well, yeah, I've read some articles in the Chronicle of Higher Education and other sources, but I haven't played with it, haven't done anything. They said, well can you jump into it and see

DOI: 10.4324/9781003770978-4

what might be there? And so, I took the summer of 2023 and just sort of immersed myself in the whole AI stuff.

Soon after that, the Center decided that they wanted to create an AI faculty fellow position, and I've served in that role for the last two and a half years. I've been doing workshops and meeting faculty 1 on 1, especially for those thinking of incorporating it into their classes.

A lot of all this for me is driven by course outcomes-does what a professor do meet their course outcomes? And more than anything else now, really what are some of the career readiness skills that the student will need? In my field, the APA has really leaned into AI in areas including how clinical psychologists and research psychologists can use it, as well as AI in education. So, I tell my students these are some of the skills you are going to need no matter what area you enter after college.

So if it makes sense, I incorporate AI into assessments—both formal ones-the more point type values—but informal assessments too where I bring a set of problems into class and then find out: are we ready to move to the next set of materials or are people still struggling in class and we need to spend more time on this segment?

RB: How does AI play a part in these assessments?

VG: Yes, so here is an example for the informal assessment. In psychology, one of the tough parts in going over a new concept is that students often do not fully understand it and have a hard time relating it to their own lives. But now I can make the case study more relatable by personalizing it to them.

In fact, sometimes I won't even create the case study until I show up in class that day with the students. This can be a bit unnerving as we don't know what the case study may actually be ahead of time and I have to think on my feet to help them generate the questions. So for example, in my class on Adolescent Development, we talk a lot about family systems, so one thing I try to do is to find a study that relates to what I learn about what the students are dealing with at the moment in their own lives, and have this as part of the prompt.

The way this works is that I start with a generic prompt that hits the concepts I want to cover. For example, if we are doing family dynamics, then I would include some systems theory content into the prompt. Then, I open it up to the class to provide me with experiences from their own family dynamics. So, a student might say, for instance, that an elderly grandparent has moved into the house and that changes the family dynamic. So now I include this into the prompt that I already started, and I can create a case study that is unique to that student's experience. Once the case has been created, we put students into small groups, and we give a set of reflection questions or sometimes AI itself may suggest questions. Once the case is set up, I can go around the room and see if they are applying the questions to this case. If they are struggling, we may need to review this more in the next class.

RB: So, the other advantage to this is that it sounds like by using AI to make the cases more relevant, it also helps with the issue of better student engagement, correct?

VG: Yes, the feedback I've been receiving from my students is that they really like the way the material is hitting their own personal experiences vs. something very generic. The other thing I can show here are the nuances about how AI does not always offer the right answers. So, they learn not to blindly use whatever comes out of the AI-you need to read through it carefully. So, I weave in this kind of AI literacy into what we do.

RB: And what about the use of AI for formal assessment?

VG: For my Intro to Psych course that I gave last fall, I gave a more traditional final exam.

I decided to let students pick a topic-either one we covered over the semester, or a different one. And their assignment was to become an expert in that area and use five resources to help them become that expert. Once they feel they have become an expert, I provide them with this prompt to input into the AI of their choice.

You are going to be an interviewer on a news magazine show like 60 minutes, and I am an expert in the particular area of (X). What I want you to do is interview me and ask me 3 questions, one question at a time, and as I answer, ask me follow ups based on my answer, and wait before going to question two until you are fully satisfied with the answer I provided for the current question.

We also tell the AI in the prompt to only ask three questions which is a good maximum, so the AI does not keep continually asking questions.

Here is an example:

> *Student's Prompt*: I am a college student in a college psychology class. Pretend like I am a guest expert on a news show. Ask me questions about classical conditioning. Ask me one question at a time and let me respond and provide me with feedback before going to the next question. Make it three different questions.

ChatGPT output: Adjusting microphone, taking on the role of a news show interviewer,

> Leaning forward attentively, ready to listen to your response
>
> Thank you for joining us today. Let me start with what many consider the foundation of classical conditioning: In your expert opinion, what made Pavlov's original experiments with dogs so groundbreaking for the field of psychology, and how did his discovery of the conditioned response change our understanding of human behavior?

They continue on with the process until all three questions are asked and answered. The student would then turn in these transcripts.

RB: So how did it work in practice?

VG: When we first tried this, I was blown away by how much ChatGPT really got into this "assignment" we gave it. And then when I looked at the questions it asked—I was blown away again, as they were the kinds of questions that if I gave essay exams, I would ask myself.

In terms of the conversation itself, students would either enter their responses on their keyboard, while others got creative and used a voice activated feature and recorded it on the site and handed that audio file in to me.

Finally, there was a set of reflection questions where they talk about matters like what the hardest part of the assignment was, what did they learn, and so on. Students said things like the questions were much more in-depth than they thought they would be, and that they had to think on their feet to apply the psychological concept to the exact question.

During the reflection, many said it was a hard but rewarding assignment.

Now could they still use a separate AI to answer the questions asked of them by the system? Sure, they could have another device to answer questions. But I think that's the case with any kind of assessment we do anymore. At some point we just have to trust the students and that they will engage in the process the way we want. Yes, some will take advantage and cheat in those areas, but there have always been those kinds of students even before AI came out.

I should mention too that while this was a traditional final, I believe a lot of the ways we do assessments now will have to change in the age of AI to more authentic projects with scaffolding and reflections.

RB: What was the main advantage of having ChatGPT ask good questions like this, versus say, a professor like you asking them the questions?

VG: One advantage is that it allowed students to pick their interest area they most wanted to know about. Had I tried to ask questions about every concept and for every student—that would be a nightmare for me to get through. But now they are having a conversation with the AI tool they choose to use, and it becomes individual to each of them. And if they need to give examples, it can be from their own lives.

RB: What were your goals for this project, and do you think you achieved them?

VG: I had a couple of goals. One was to be able to talk to students closely and more directly about AI. Actually, it is in classes where instructors are ignoring it and hoping it goes away where I think students are using AI the most. So one big thing for me is to talk to them-when it is appropriate to use AI, and when it is not appropriate.

In the realm of AI and critical thinking, I think AI can be very valuable to *help* critical thinking if it is used in the proper way and prompted the right way. Sure, it can write a paper if I just prompt it and it may be good enough to get a student through a class. But if a student realizes they can use AI more thoughtfully to ask matters like—am I missing something? Do you have suggestions on how to organize this material, and so on—then it is not writing for me, it is now more like an assistant, and I see it then as a very valuable tool.

Of course, even with that kind of use, I think there are various levels of opinion of faculty as to what constitutes cheating.

My other goal was to use AI to help achieve course outcomes, specifically around the areas of communication and knowledge of concepts. I find these ways I've been using AI more engaging and personal for students. I remember a virtual conference I attended in the summer of 2023 put on by both faculty and students and one of my favorite parts was a panel of students on how they were using the technology. One faculty said to the students, "can you see this from our point of view, and how it can scare us?" One student replied, "no offense to you but if students are cheating on your assignments it's not because of some new technology it's probably either because your assignment is boring or has very little relevance to what I am doing in college."

And that sort of hit me as I went back to see how I used to assess assignments and realized that some of mine could fit that description:—boring or not relevant. And even when they were relevant, I did not do a good job of connecting to why it matters to their work after they graduate.

Ultimately, I think AI is less of a tech issue and more of a pedagogy issue. It has forced me to rethink the goals of education, what we want students to be able to accomplish over the course of a semester. Is giving students a 75-question multiple-choice exam really what we want them to get out of the course?

RB: OK but what about pure writing assignments? So, let's say you were teaching a first year writing class and as part of that you did have to assign a paper on a historical event. How would you introduce it in a way that would enable the student to do good research, make connections, analyze things, and then express it all clearly. How would the use of AI fit in here?

VG: So first, I think I would probably break the process down into smaller steps. As opposed to just turning the paper in at the end.

I'll be grading the final paper, but I also would have initial steps they go through, and one of the things that I think I would build in as part of those initial steps would be verbal feedback. I would use the flipped classroom where students would work on a project while in the classroom and during those sessions, I would bring each student up to me and say you worked on this, how did you do it? It would become apparent at that point if they were just offloading everything to an AI to research and write. So in my syllabus in fact, I state that anything you do is subject to a verbal review.

I would also like to talk a bit about how it's OK to use AI but here is how to use it at these different steps or functions. For instance, did you use it to fix grammar?—that's OK, or did you use it as a brainstorming or organizational tool? I'd be fine with that. So I'd be turning the paper more into a process rather than an end product that you would simply turn in when due.

RB: Do you think that it's ever possible to give students enough self-learning skills, discipline, knowledge, and meta-awareness that they can make their own decision to willingly choose not to use AI when they think it is not useful, helpful, or appropriate?

VG: Yes, I think this knowledge and perspective could be built into educational experience. One is to show a fellow faculty member how to show their students when a certain AI usage would align with the students' goals. For example, say a chemistry professor says to me, as an AI fellow, how can I incorporate AI into my classes? I may then ask them how are chemists actually using it in the field now? Maybe you should hook up with someone in the field and have them come in and talk to your students about how it is being used in the field, along with what are poor or dangerous uses, so it would be an educational experience for the student.

RB: So that is an AI usage incentive or motivation that would align to their goals. But what about students that don't want to use AI?

VG: Yes, I have a number of students that are saying they are against AI. Some are in education and will become teachers, and for them it is an academic integrity issue. Others say it is an equity issue, arguing that they or other classmates can't afford the paid versions, while some of my classmates are able to, and so can do much more, creating things that those with the free versions cannot come up with. Others say they are against AI because of their environmental concerns.

RB: What would you do if one of your students did not want to use AI?

VG: I would probably talk to them a little bit more, flush out their thinking. Some of this will come down to the kind of relationships you create with your students. I am very much into building relationships—I get to know them well, and they know me—I talk about all kinds of things about my own life, family life—and so I think that I feel that I have a trust and strong relationship between myself and the students. Other faculty, well I know in large institutions or large lecture hall classes or online, it may be harder. I'm fortunate that my largest classes are no more than about 35 students.

RB: Finally, any advice or dos and don'ts for other faculty that may want to try something similar to what you did here?

VG: Yes, start small. Maybe just try it with one assignment. Try doing this yourself too as if you were a student. Be sure to have the reflection questions and get a lot of feedback from the students as to what you should do differently, the next time around. Think of them as your partner in this endeavor.

Vincent Granito is a Professor of Psychology at Lorain County Community College and an AI and Assessment Faculty Fellow focused on ethical, learning-centered uses of artificial intelligence in higher education. He also served as an AI/OER Fellow with the Institute for the Study of Knowledge Management in Education (ISKME), where his work investigated how AI can enhance the development, adaptation, and sustainability of open educational resources.

Contact: vgranito@lorainccc.edu

Dr. Lynette Pretorius, Lecturer, School of Teaching and Learning, Faculty of Education, Monash University, Melbourne, Australia

We are trying to move beyond students being marked on how pretty their English writing is—we don't feel our job is to teach them to write pretty English but to teach them to think for themselves.

To build long-term career readiness, Dr. Pretorius implements a comprehensive university-wide framework where AI usage is completely permitted (unless explicitly prohibited for a specific pedagogical reason) and structured around disciplined AI acknowledgment rubrics, For undergraduate students, she replaces high-stakes summative exams with heavily scaffolded, small formative tasks—such as having an AI generate a baseline response that students must actively critique, evaluate, and orally defend in class to prove their individual mastery. For students who object to using AI, she says that if as an ethically minded person, they have chosen not to use AI, which is a totally reasonable choice to take because that is part of being a good digital citizen. Our policy is then we need to provide a version of the assignment that does not use AI.

RB: So, if I understand your area of interest in AI in the classroom, you have been doing work on how AI could help spur higher-order cognitive thinking correct?

LP: Yes, I would say that is the case. My work is AI literacy focused and after students become AI literate they start working with it as a collaborative knowledge partner, so that at that point the AI can be used to build critical thinking versus just what it can do for you. But they can't get to the point where AI can supplant their critical thinking, and not just replace it, until they have become AI literate.

RB: What is involved in this effort?

LP: Here at Monash University, we were one of the forerunners on how AI can be integrated into the classroom. We adopted this policy early on as there is no point in stopping it so we might as well help students learn to use it well. So, the university is doing a full programmatic alignment to teach these skills at various levels to integrate it into different assessment tasks at different stages, and in different ways to help students learn.

I teach at different unit levels. I teach an AI Master Class mostly for the graduate research students, but I also teach AI as part of the referencing workshops for the undergraduates as well as for master students about how to be AI literate and how to teach it as well. And the core unit I teach is a very niche research methods class on how to do autoethnographic research, and there AI is embedded as a form of data generation to help students reflect on their own experience (For more details see https://doi.org/10.26180/25965178)

RB: So, you permit AI usage for those that are AI literate.

LP: Yes, if there is an essay project, for example, students choose their own topic, and the class is set up so they can refine their topics, think about how things fit together and unless it has been explicitly prohibited, students can use AI whatever way they want as long as it is clearly acknowledged. And we teach them how to do AI usage acknowledgment properly. The university has a policy that if you do not want students to use AI you need a pedagogical reason to justify to the university why they are not allowed to use it.

In another unit they learn how to develop their own lesson plan. First, they write it on their own and then they put it into AI to get feedback on it and the process continues. It is not banned after that first student creation, as we want to show them how they can use it to elevate their thinking.

The other thing is we are trying to move beyond students being marked on how pretty their English writing is—we don't feel our job to teach them to write pretty English but to teach them to think for themselves. If they use AI to make their English nice and pretty that is fine as long as they acknowledge it properly.

RB: So, it seems the university's teaching policy and bigger picture is to develop critical thinking and as long as something does not take away from it, that is OK.

LP: Yes, and the bigger picture I think is that students need to know how to use AI well when they go into the workforce whatever that may be. So the graduate attribute here is that they need to be AI literate in their discipline. And so, across the university, in all faculties, there are different ways in which people have incorporated it in to teach the students how to use it well rather than to use it just to do stuff for you.

RB: I imagine though you still have students that go to a chatbot because of time pressures, a focus on grades, a lack of maturity, and so on, right?

LP: Yes, certainly our students range from straight out of high school to PhD and certainly those just out of high school are not that mature yet and we see more of that —it's much less of a problem in the higher levels.

The younger ones are less mature and may not do what they are supposed to do because it is easier, but it is then incumbent on the educator to design assessment tasks with good practices embedded. We have, for instance, long moved away from the summative final exam. And we are the faculty of Education, so we like to do pedagogically sound things. First-year undergraduates tend to have small formative assessments, like writing a paragraph, getting feedback on that paragraph, then building the paragraph into an argument, presenting that argument in an oral in the class, then writing their final argument. So, it is about embedding the skills across the unit or course and changing the assessments to ensure that they programmatically develop skills.

For the undergrads there's a lot more small, little assessment tasks. They are told, so you got ChatGPT to write your paragraph, you wrote nice English sentences, but this and this and this is problematic, so how can you do that part better next time? There will be several units where, for example, they get the language model to generate a response to a question, and then in the class, their actual assessment is to analyze and evaluate that output, and suggest areas where they can be improved. This showcases how the AIs are not perfect and can have problems. The assessment is on critiquing that work.

RB: What are some other ways AI is being utilized?

LP: In the master's unit I teach, the formatting of the AI acknowledgment is one of the criteria on the rubric. And they get marks for doing it properly and we spend time in the class teaching them these things.

We also have a large international cohort, so there is a lot of concern among students there about their linguistic capacity and if they are writing good enough English. So when they learn about AI and that they are allowed to use it, they are keen to use it to make their writing better.

One way it was being used by the students themselves that surprised me, was that one week there was a really cognitively complex topic, and I saw a student looking at a computer screen while I was talking and it was displaying a live translation of me into Mandarin. I thought, all right I am OK with that. If she can't understand my topic as it is too complex in English, and she can get it to translate to a language she can understand that is fine with me. This seemed like Star Trek Level technology, but now I see it happening more and more.

RB: For the younger students, the first or second year students, after they have taken an AI Literacy courses, was there a particular AI aspect of the course that you think has actually made a difference in helping a student voluntarily choose to eschew going to AI if they know it is not going to be good for them?

LP: Two things. So, for the lower level students, the AI literacy is combined with the referencing and academic integrity workshop-students do know about not plagiarizing, but are not sure what it all means now, but this helps and puts it all together. This way they know what they are allowed and not allowed to do.

Also, a key part of the class that can lead some to choose not to use AI is the segment on the ethical dimension of AI literacy. We argue that to be AI literate you need to understand the ethical dimensions, and we have developed a whole framework. One of which is to consider the social impacts-this includes perpetuation of biases, increases in the digital divide between the ones that have the skills vs those that don't, and the environmental effects-impacts on sustainability.

And the main reason a student may choose not to use AI is its environmental impact. Some of them also have the bias issue, but most of the time it is the environmental impact, because, you know, young people are very concerned about the environment and for good reasons. And if, as an ethically minded person they have chosen not to use AI that is a totally reasonable choice to take because that is part of being a good digital citizen. Our policy is that we need to provide a version of the assignment that does not use AI,

RB: Do any students choose not to use it because they are concerned about the development of their critical thinking?

LP: I think—yes, for some. When I start the class, I ask them what they know about AI and their concerns, and there is a prevailing perception that they might lose their capacity to think for themselves and to think deeply. Some of them even after you teach how it can elevate their thinking, will still say that "I want to use my own way of thinking." Others are naturally resistant to technology, for good reasons, or—some who have always done it a certain way want to continue in that manner, and some are concerned that they will lose the ability to think for themselves.

RB: Is there any good way to actually study to find out how successful a specific AI-enabled assignment or assessment was, to discover how the students actually did or did not use AI and if some went around the guidelines of how to use it and in fact did just turn to it for answers.

LP: You're never going to find them all since some will lie but there is a lot of research in Australia on students perceptions and use of AI. There's a major research group here called the *Centre for Research in Assessment and Digital Learning (CRADLE*) at Deakin University doing these kinds of studies.

Here I've looked at this issue on a smaller scale. There is an anonymous survey we have sent after they had their marks in and are in the next unit. And we interviewed them and asked them about their decision making: questions like, so why did you do this and why did you not do this, and we give them the opportunity to share. Other things people have done are to embed reflections into the assessment tasks over the semester, so they are required to reflect on how they used AI, which parts was useful, which were not useful and what they learned in the process. Some faculty ask them to include their AI conversations as appendix. But the prevailing research is showing that overall the students are making informed decisions and being quite judicious in their choices as to what they want to do, why they are using it or not using it, and how they are incorporating it in their work so that it doesn't do the work for them.

RB: Is there anything we didn't discuss that you feel is important to mention?

LP: Yes, so critical thinking is one of the higher order thinking skills, and in our AI literacy framework, one thing we discuss is social emotional awareness. Our engagement with technology—and this is not a new concept—is underpinned by emotional thoughts and feelings about things. This is the same with our emotional reactions to AI. So social emotional skills need to be developed so that people can understand where their initial responses come from and can then think more critically on the choice they are making rather than instantly say it is the greatest thing or it is evil. It's important to reflect on your own emotional responses and how that has caused you to say something and how you might be able to think about it more critically.

I see this on social media all the time, and you will always get someone who complains and goes on a rant about how evil AI is, and will take all jobs and destroy the world. You can see it in the way they are responding to it that they are responding from a purely emotional spot but don't even realize that they are.

Dr. Lynette Pretorius is an award-winning educator and researcher. She draws on her interdisciplinary expertise to create inclusive and transformative learning environments. Her research focuses on doctoral education, AI literacy, research literacy, academic identity, and student wellbeing.

Contact: https://www.lynettepretorius.com/

Michelle Kassorla, PhD, Associate Professor, English, Perimeter College at Georgia State University, Atlanta, GA

> *If you ignore AI, you invite cheating—and if you are obsessed with cheating, you are not focused on learning. You need to take off the policeman's cap and put down your whistle and teach. You're a teacher, not a policeman.*

To adapt to an environment where AI can effortlessly simulate finished schoolwork, Dr. Kassorla co-designed a curriculum that explicitly moves away from high-stakes summative grading to evaluate the *process* of learning through continuous formative assessments. Instead of shielding students from the technology, she requires them to construct custom prompts from scratch and submit their complete AI chat logs, grading them on their direct human agency in critiquing, training, and correcting the chatbot when its responses fail to match assignment guidelines. And to prevent automated cheating and verify authentic comprehension, she implements real-time Socratic AI tutoring for paragraph mechanics, updates her grading rubrics to explicitly reward a distinct "human voice" and rigorous fact-checking, and mandates "reflective footnotes" throughout the writing.

RB: Please give me some background on your initiative and how it came about?

MK: It was June 2023 and I was watering plants on my porch when my colleague, Eugenia Novokshanova called me up and said

> As you know, I am a specialist in multimodal writing, and you are very interested in putting AI into your classes. Maybe we can combine our efforts and work together to make a template that is just for you and me.

That was when the Multimodal AI Project started, and we worked together to build Composition 1 with AI.

The first thing we initially tried to do was to teach against AI but we realized that was a losing proposition so we decided to leverage AI for critical thinking.

So, we redesigned our classes for AI. And we realized that everything our education experts were telling us to do for years we needed to put into place—that means first of all to teach using formative not summative assessment. We also decided to teach around what an employer wants when it comes to using AI. What we determined was that employers would want students to be able to follow directions, to sound human and know how to fact-check. And students have to be transparent with their use of AI.

RB: Tell me more about how you came to the determination that you can't teach against AI.

MK: AI will always be there and if you try to prohibit it, students will find another way; and you don't want to start an arms race. Also, AI detectors are completely ineffectual.

And along the way we did have some doubts, were we wrong to teach with AI? But then we realized there was no other way. If you ignore IA, you invite cheating—and if you are obsessed with cheating, you are not focused on learning. You need to take off the policeman's cap and put down your whistle and teach. You're a teacher, not a policeman.

RB: Tell me more about the details of your strategy.

MK: Mike Kentz [an educator, researcher, writer and Adjunct Faculty at Fairleigh Dickinson University] came up with a great idea—to read students' AI chat logs. So, in our English 1102 when our students do AI lessons, we check to make sure they completed those lessons and that they interacted appropriately with AI by checking their chat logs. We use AI to help them with one of the parts of a research problem that always is a challenge for students-helping them narrow their topic. So, we looked at their chat logs on how they did this.

So, we would ask them to share their original idea or topic—and then use AI to help them with their revised topic and share their chat log with us. Students thought we were looking mainly at their original and revised topic, but what we were really focusing on was that chat log.

RB: What were you looking for in the chat logs?

MK: We looked for certain specific things. One was that they followed the directions of the assignment. But the most important thing was that the students showed agency; we share our prompts with our students. Lots of professors and teachers put their prompts into a CustomGPT or a Gem "bot," because it is easier to do and the students don't have to mess with cutting and pasting prompts in, but we don't do that as they need to understand what a prompt is and how they work-and they need to understand what we are telling the AI to do. And if the AI did not follow the prompt—the students needed to call out the AI, showing their agency in training that AI. We wanted to see if they were telling the AI that what it provided was not what we wanted, or it was too obsequious. So, they are graded on how they showed they were critical and applying critical thinking with that AI-that is how their grades are based. They have to push the AI as hard as they can.

Here is the prompt provided to a student using the AI-Assisted tutor to revise an academic paragraph:

> I am working on a supporting paragraph for a research paper, and I need help improving my supporting paragraph step by step. Act as a tutor and guide me through the revision process. Do not write or rewrite anything for me! Instead, ask me to guide questions and give suggestions that allow me to improve my own writing. Assess the paragraph in four specific areas step by step, one area at a time.
>
> 1 Clarity and strength of the topic sentence: Does the topic sentence clearly introduce the main idea of the paragraph, and is it strong enough to guide the rest of the paragraph? If not, ask me questions to help me strengthen the sentence, and guide me through revising this part up to one to three times. Do not write the sentence for me!
> 2 Relevance of evidence: Are the quotations and paraphrases relevant, specific, and insightful to support the paragraph's main idea? If not, ask me questions to help me strengthen my quotes, and guide me through revising this part up to one to three times. Do not write sentences for me!
> 3 Integration of quotes using signal phrases: Are signal phrases effectively introducing quotations by providing information about the speaker? Are the quotes properly cited in MLA format? Are the quotes properly punctuated? If not, ask me questions to help me clarify the details, and guide me through revising this part up to one to three times. Do not move on to the next section until I have successfully revised the integration of all quotations.
> 4 Depth of analysis: Does my analysis of quoted evidence go beyond just repetition and stating facts? Does it provide a complex understanding and elaborate insightfully on the evidence from sources? If not, ask me questions to help me clarify the details, and guide me through revising this part up to one to three times. Do not write sentences for me!
>
> To make your recommendations clear, give specific examples based on the content of my paragraph, but do not rewrite actual revision for me. To begin our tutoring session, prompt me with "Please provide your original paragraph below and wait for me to enter my paragraph."

We also used AI to produce Socratic-style tutoring. They would write a paragraph, the AI would look at it, and ask them questions, and the student responds and the AI integrates their responses into the paragraph. So, we then expanded the use of the tutor to show them how to write a proper academic paragraph: they would submit one and then AI would ask key questions like what your signal phrase is, who wrote this particular statement, what are their affiliations, and so on. The AI might also ask about one of the quotations in the paragraph and ask the student to analyze it and ask questions like what does that quote mean, why is it the right quote for your paper?

RB: So, these kinds of good questions that the AI are asking—they seem like the kinds of questions a good human teacher would ask. What are the advantages of having an AI do it?

MK: We don't have the time to individually tutor each student, but the AI does. So, we say read the prompt and make sure the AI sticks with the prompt as we will read the chat logs later. And we tell the AI to keep asking them for prompts until it is correct—it is a long process—some students said they spent hours doing this as they did not realize how hard it was to write. So, when we got these paragraphs back the student response was overwhelming-they said they did not like all the hard work, but they said they learned a lot and saw the value of it.

Basically, we handed the mechanics of the process to the machine. So, then what is left is human agency and voice, and that is what we wanted to promulgate: agency and voice.

This also meant that we needed to redo our assessments as well. Our previous rubric used to look at mechanical aspects like spelling, punctuation, paragraph formation, and so on. But now in my rubrics there are things like "do you have a strong human voice?" "Could I tell your individual agency?" "Was everything factual and did you check it to make sure it was factual." And how efficient were you—were you able to get this work done in the time allotted? So, we took those values that we started with what an employer would want and applied it directly to our rubrics.

RB: What were some other innovations you added?

MK: The last thing was something Eugenia had done for years but she never realized how brilliant it was. While the idea of student reflection on what one learned in a class at its conclusion is not uncommon, what she did was integrate an ongoing metacognitive reflection practice for the student to think about what they were doing and why *while* they were doing it. She created the process of what she called "reflective footnotes" which was active cognitive reflection, to occur as the students were writing or creating something.

What they do is stop and write down their thinking about their process and choices they made as they were doing it: This can work for any subject too—think about chemistry. An ongoing reflection could be, for instance, why did I choose to add this chemical at this time in the lab and not after another chemical. What was the purpose of doing it at this point?

[Note: see Chapter 4 for a discussion on the use of reflection "wrappers" to initiate self-regulated learning among students while engaged in their assignment]

RB: And this is related to AI, right?

MK: Yes, because if the students cannot describe their process, they did not do their work.

RB: What is the mechanism for them to do these notes as they are researching and writing?

MK: We tell them in 10 pages we want 5 footnotes. They can decide where to put them—it's about their process and their understanding. And we ask them focused metacognitive questions after the paper is completed too.

RB: Do you feel you have achieved the goal you originally set out to achieve? Are there areas you feel you fell short or if you were to do this again you would do something differently?

MK: We were constantly adjusting, doing things differently, adjusting our lessons. We'd get a lot of reflections—these were not just for our students but for us too! We needed to know if things were working the way we want—it's a brand new area and nobody really knows what they are doing-this area is constantly changing and everything is different every day.

I have also been looking at Blooms taxonomy again. What I realized is Bloom's taxonomy is completely useless for the age of AI because it assumes that "create" is at the top of the pyramid. But with AI we create *first*-which turns the whole model on the head-you have the students create (a picture, poem, song) and then we all talk about how you evaluate that. What kind of thing do we consider to be good and bad? And then, how can you analyze what you've done and change it? Then how can you apply that to the understanding of your analysis and what is the evaluation? So, working backward: through that, rewriting things as you go, so starting with the AI product, every step that you take brings you toward remembering, and remembering is the last step in this process, instead of the first step, as it would be in Bloom's. In engaging this process, you have worked through the process of eliminating AI and increasing human agency at every step. When you get to remembering, that is entirely human.

RB: Stepping back now when you began this project, what were the main barriers or objections you faced along the way? Any pushback? How did you overcome them-or are some still not fully resolved?

MK: When Eugenie and I started we called it our AI Multimodal project and worked it through our classes, we had a lot of anger from our department from individual professors who thought we were teaching our students to cheat. They did not understand what we were doing or how we were doing it, even though they did not know what we were doing. They would not even say hello to us in the hallway, and it was like we were the pariahs of the department. They asked me to create a new module for composition, but they said but "NO AI"

But this year, in this semester, suddenly, it's, could you go in and change that template to include AI? And they're telling everyone to use AI. So, I think that everything has really changed starting this year, that everyone, it's all Pro-AI.

RB: What else is coming up on the horizon that is worth noting here?

MK: Now there are AI agents, they affect the college. One danger area is that Agentic AI scan go into our LMS systems, pretend it's a student, complete all the work in the class and turn it in and there is no interaction with a student at all. The student just starts them out, and the agents go in and take everything.

[For more on AI agents, and specific strategies from Kassorla, see Chapter 5.]

Michelle Kassorla, PhD, an Associate Professor at Georgia State University, Perimeter College, has more than 30 years of experience teaching writing. She has been teaching with AI in every class since Fall 2023. Since then, she has shared practical tips on teaching with AI on her LinkedIn, in keynotes, for conference presentations, and as a participant in national higher education organizations.

Contact: mkassorla@gsu.edu

Perry Samson, Professor Emeritus, Atmospheric Sciences, University of Michigan, Ann Arbor, MI

Kevyn Collins-Thompson, Associate Professor, School of Information, and Electrical Engineering and Computer Science, University of Michigan, Ann Arbor, MI

> *The existence of AI has made it harder for us to know what students are actually learning. Now we can know what process they go through... something you wouldn't get if you're just giving out a paper exam or such.*
>
> *Perry Samson*

Perry Samson and Kevyn Collins-Thompson describe their development and use of *LearningClues*, an automated educational platform that ingests course-specific materials from an LMS to generate interactive, real-time voice and text chatbot conversations that guide students through dense academic materials without directly revealing the answers. This framework is designed to have students verbally demonstrate comprehension of their assignments during recorded, low-stakes Socratic check-ins that automatically log student progress against an instructor's rubric.

Note: As this was a discussion with two people, the initials PS are for responses from Perry Samson and KCT for Kevyn Collins-Thompson.

RB: So, let's begin with the description of the presentation you gave at the 2025 Educause Conference. Here is the description of your LearningClues project published in the program:

> *LearningClues leverages generative AI to provide private, session-specific insights derived from class transcripts, slides, and teaching materials. The system maps learning objectives, highlights instructional strategies, generates sample student questions, and flags potential areas of confusion. Pilot results show how this feedback supports reflective teaching and course design while respecting instructor autonomy.*

KCT: Yes, our system can crawl the class materials in the LMS and produce questions. The thing we are particularly excited about is that it operates as a kind of gamified conversation that gets the students to engage and reason through problems. The instructor defines a structured conversation and a rubric with the AI. The authoring tool lets the instructor define the challenge, specify the rubric by which the students will be evaluated, and define the nature and level of expertise of the interrogator. The students also get feedback, which is integrated into the LMS.

Here is a demo of how it works.

[At this point, I was able to view a demo of the product-see the below screen shot and audio transcript]

Here you will see that the instructor provides students with a weekly reading, and this one I am showing here (see Figure 3.1) is a computer science paper titled "Attention is All You Need." The students can engage in

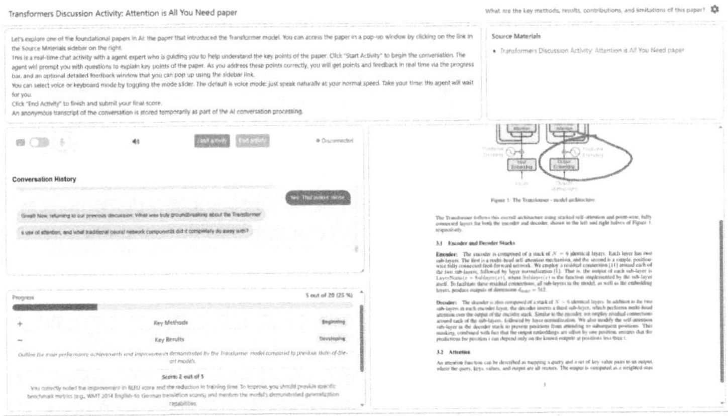

Figure 3.1 The students can engage in real time, guided conversation in a natural way with an expert about anything that is in a document, including figures and tables.

real time, guided conversation in a natural way with an expert about anything that is in that paper, including figures and tables.

And a rubric is created in advance that directs how the conversation proceeds. So, for example, for this one, I created four key points to engage the student: describe the key methods in the paper, the results, the contributions, and the limitations.

And then, as the student goes through the various conversations and activities, as they hit the various points correctly, things will light up, their progress moves ahead to the next one and so on.

(Chatbot voice)

(Chatbot) Hi, I'm Dr. Susan Carlin, but you can call me Susan. This activity is all about exploring the key aspects of the Attention is All You Need paper. We'll be covering the key methods, results, contributions, and limitations, but feel free to address them in any order you like. My goal is to help you really dig into the paper and understand it better.

To start, the paper introduces the transformer model, which relies entirely on attention mechanisms. Before we delve deeper, can you recall what the paper mentions about why attention mechanisms are so important in sequence modeling?

(Student): Well, they... they let you capture, interaction between... between any pair of words in a given context. And that helps the system develop a rich semantic model of the text.

(Chatbot) That's a great start. So, attention mechanisms can look at relationships between words, no matter how far apart they are.

(Student): Actually, before we continue, could you help explain Figure 3.1 to me? Because that was something in the paper that I really didn't get.

(Chatbot) Of course. Figure 3.1 is a high-level view of the transformer's architecture, showing how the encoder and decoder are connected. Looking at Figure 3.1, can you describe in your own words what the encoder does in the transformer model? What is its main role?

(Student) I have no idea.

(Chatbot) No worries, let's break it down.

RB: So just to clarify, when you discuss that the student is conversing with an expert, here you are referring not to a person, but to the chatbot correct?

KCT: Yes, the chatbot has all the information about the materials, the goals and some information about the student. The interrogator stimulates a conversation (verbal or typed) and responds to student comments to guide the student to successfully complete the assignment.

And this can be a graded activity or it could be a participatory one. It's meant to be more informal, and not meant for high-stakes situations. I've deployed this as a pilot in my machine learning classes, and the students who've tried it appreciated the communicative way to work through a complex problem, as well as the real-time voice interaction which provided a very natural, low-effort modality.

And Perry has been developing other applications of this technology. For example, he created a medical use, one where the student practices doing role-playing as a physician diagnosing measles. I showed it to a doctor who happens to be a student in one of our programs, and they said, wow, this is incredible.

And there are other applications. There's a sort of Socratic question asking one, and there's role-playing activities, and others can include language learning and shadowing activities.

RB: What is the foundation of this system? What was it built on?

KCT: I created a client-server framework that is based on a real-time multimedia streaming framework called Pipecat from daily.co. [A developer platform for real-time voice, video, and AI integration.] Pipecat handles all of it and creates a virtual room for the student to engage with the chatbot. In the future, we want to have multiple students join a virtual room. Right now, it's just a one-on-one with the bot.

Internally, the server that sits in the middle works like a conductor, calling out to all of these very high-quality services to do text-to-speech, speech-to-text, and other AI-based functions. Underneath it all in the background and in parallel, generative AI (currently Gemini) provides support for managing the interactions with the student and tasks, like conversational turn-taking and scoring.

RB: Regarding the use of Gemini, is the data and domain of what the chatbot is drawing from a limited, constrained domain just of the course materials, or does Gemini also reach out to pull from its general knowledge base as well?

KCT: The instructor defines the expert knowledge base (the course materials, texts, conversations, etc.) for the chatbot, which provides critical context consisting of course materials or relevant external resources. The chatbot will automatically prefer information that comes from this knowledge base, which will restrict the structure of the conversation. It is also constrained that it won't give the answer. Instead. it is designed to get the student to describe concepts in their own words.

RB: There are a lot of ed tech companies out there now that are trying to do things similar. What would you say is most distinctive that sets you apart?

PS: I can jump in here for a second. One distinction is that we've built an entire system that automatically ingests everything in a course, so it knows what's in the LMS, regardless of whether you use Blackboard, Canvas, D2L, or another platform. We know, also if you have recorded course classes, or if you have video, and this is ingested as well. And so all this can be brought to bear as part of the conversation and in the context of one's course, so that the instructor can feel confident that the responses the system is giving reflect the material that they have required.

KCT: And because we have that deep course context, it allows us to do things like design activities that make use of the course context that a generic LLM wouldn't necessarily have.

This also gets to some of the AI resilience properties of these kinds of things. Students can ask questions about the lecture that just happened yesterday, or the homework that they submitted, questions that would be difficult or impossible for a generic AI to answer.

RB: Is this system designed for online, in person and/or hybrid classrooms?

KCT: I would say it could be used for either. But it works best with online classes as they are video-centric, but it doesn't have to work that way.

RB: When looking at this project as a whole, how would you define success, specifically from a learning perspective?

KCT: First, I would say success would look like real actionable insights for instructors on where students are still struggling and to identify where the gaps are in the course. From the student's point of view, I would see success as better retention of material and better engagement. We have interaction data that show that students are actually engaging with the weekly readings that we want them to, and asking questions.

RB: And how would you actually find and use data to determine answers to those questions?

KCT: Well, the system has the built in capacity to run randomized controlled trials, so if we're interested in how the capabilities of the system may or may not affect certain variables or outcomes, we can do that automatically.

Also I'm in the School of Information at Michigan, and we like to use mixed methods, so I can combine data analytics, analyzing interaction data, online interaction data, along with small usability studies in a lab that are highly instrumented. When we do the analysis of interaction data to get at engagement we can anonymously, but in depth, see what are students asking about and in a much more fine-grained manner about how they're responding to the different points and on a scale we haven't been able to get before in a class. So, I would say all three modes would be important to get a full picture of what is happening. In addition we can do interviews with stakeholders and get their feedback.

And we can also do a delayed post-test in the next course. They're more challenging to run, but we can get at retention that way.

PS: There's one other aspect we have not mentioned and that is we can track students over time. So if they're in a program like Kevyn's, we know what courses they've taken in the past, and when conversations happen the system could bring up material from courses they've been in before, because as you well know, students don't always learn the first time. The idea is by knowing the content they've been exposed to along the way, we can reinforce that as they move forward through these kinds of tools.

RB: Are there any student privacy considerations at play here?

PS: Well, we're very FERPA compliant, and while we obviously know what students said, we don't record or report that back to even the instructor.

The instructor is going to get only summaries of the results, such as where did students in general have issues, and what misconceptions came up.

We are also working on a research project in which we would de-identify the data and then be able to share it so people could do research on the designs and process of learning. But we obviously really need to control access to the data.

And all this gets to this gets at a point that the existence of AI has made it harder for us to know what students are actually learning. Now we can know what process they go through it this activity. And we at least have more information about what process did they go through, something you wouldn't get if you're just giving out a paper exam or such.

RB: What about when students are no longer in the classroom? Don't we still have the problem of students that choose, for whatever not so good reason, to turn to a general AI instead with the temptation that it will be an easier way to finish an assignment or essay?

KCT: That's a good point, but one of the ways that we are going to be using this is that there's an activity that will allow an instructor to go to an essay like you just mentioned to create a follow-up discussion activity around what the student submitted. So then, the student has to show that they understand what they turned in.

I see these kinds of follow-up activities, as kind of a quick check that can just give feedback on whether they understood what they submitted. We haven't implemented that quite yet, but we're on the verge of making that available, and see that as potentially a very important follow-up type of activity for instructors.

But, its true like you said, like, there's nothing that prevents people from doing that [going to a general AI on their own]

In some sense, I don't care if they copied and pasted it. If they understand everything they submitted, great. We're not trying to create a plagiarism detector, or what have you.

But I think ultimately the assessment, obviously, is under the control of the instructor, and people are doing some things like, for example, having students keep a log of their work on the essay, you know to show your thinking while you're developing the themes, and, there will be record of your progress, and so forth. And they're required to submit updates to that as the assignment continues.

RB: A lot of what you are doing is creating a system that optimizes what a good teacher could or should be doing such as by asking engaging Socratic type questions and reflections. Looking out say, five years, are there inherent capacities that humans are better at and will retain that you think realistically cannot be replaced by AI?

KCT: Well, it will be very interesting to see what happens in the next five or ten years here. I tend to break this down into two main areas: socio-technical aspects, meaning, how people interact on a personal level and topical expertise. I do feel that humans will continue to do a better job of synthesizing the broader contexts, from their life experience, and knowledge of all of the contexts around the program or a student.

I mean, I guess at some level, you could imagine that all that context could be part of a generative AI system, but I still feel that human experts will be able to integrate world knowledge in a way that won't be done by generative AI for some time, because it doesn't have world models, it doesn't really understand cause and effect, especially for recent or unusual things. I think humans will remain better at this because of their improved ability to generalize, and to think, to be able to infer to new situations.

RB: An educator who was skeptical of AI as a replacement for a teacher said something to me once that stood out to me. She said that technology is not going to know, for instance, that say, Jimmy's father just went to prison, or Heather's mother has cancer, or that another student's parents are getting divorced, and so on and those are the things that we as teachers do know and can integrate into how we relate and teach each student.

KCT: Yes, I agree with that person and that's exactly the kind of situations I had in mind when I was talking about synthesizing context.

RB: Finally, is there anything else we didn't discuss that you'd like to mention?

KCT: Yes, one big thing lacking I see right now is an organized method for testing these tools before they're deployed. We are severely lacking in AI education sandboxes and benchmarks. There are not enough resources now to validate tools that are being released in classrooms. Yes, there's a lot of effort on things like low-level security which is, of course, important, but there's a lot less on AI safety, meaning that AI-powered assessment tools like Assessment Clues require rigorous, standardized testing environments and benchmarks to ensure they are valid, reliable, and fair before being deployed in real classrooms.

Perry Samson is an entrepreneur and Professor Emeritus at the University of Michigan, and Co-Founder/CEO of LearningClues, an AI platform for course-grounded learning and assessment. He has spent over four decades advancing educational technology, including founding Weather Underground and LectureTools, both of which achieved successful exits.

Contact: samson@learningclues.com

Kevyn Collins-Thompson is Co-Founder and CTO of LearningClues and an Associate Professor of Information and Computer Science at the University of Michigan. Formerly a researcher at Microsoft Research, he specializes in intelligent information retrieval, AI-driven learning systems, and data science education.

Contact: kevynct@umich.edu

Peter Bodary, PhD, clinical associate professor, University of Michigan, Ann Arbor, MI

The whole purpose of our classes should be about learning, not about the grade. I think in Canada and in the US students are just so ingrained to feel that the whole purpose of school is to get the grade, to get to the next step. And that's really become a very unfortunate thing in that we have trained all students to believe well, I can earn the grade by pasting in some information that I never read.

To optimize exam preparation and target student knowledge gaps, Dr. Boday utilizes *Maizey*, a University of Michigan-developed Retrieval-Augmented Generation (RAG) model, to power a local, learning theory-grounded "Wolverine Tutor" chatbot that queries students using purely course-specific slides and learning objectives rather than open-web knowledge. Operating strictly as a non-punitive, optional Socratic partner, the system tracks which of the 40+ unit objectives a student has attempted or mastered via an adaptive natural-language interface, forcing them to type out comprehensive conceptual arguments rather than picking multiple-choice options. Finally, it leverages interactive RAG models to simulate 24/7 virtual clients and patients for realistic, real-world case study practice.

RB: In my discussion with Perry Samson and Kevyn Collins-Thompson at the University of Michigan, they suggested I speak with you in how you are also using an inhouse AI as a question asking tutor for your classes. Can you say a bit more about this?

PB: Sure, while I'm not currently using their Learning Clues system, I have been using a University of Michigan developed RAG ["Retrieval Augmented Generation"] model called Maizey that provides the system with prompts to connect to our own "local" material (Figure 3.2).

We built this to work as a Socratic tool, so we put our course materials and lectures into a Google Folder, and Maizey is connected to the materials and we developed system prompts to decide how Maizey should respond. We decided not to make it an "answer giving" machine but designed it to talk to students in a Socratic method relating to objectives in the course. We used this in our 300-level Exercise Physiology (MVS 340) course.

Our version is called Wolverine Tutor which was developed by my colleagues Qingqing Yan, who has a Master of Arts in learning design and technology from Michigan, and Giselle Aronoff, who is a recent graduate from one of our programs in kinesiology, which is called Movement Science. The system was built on learning theories to make it maximally beneficial for the student.

This, I think, is part of the magic of this chatbot, that it is really grounded in these learning theories.

RB: So how does it work in practice?

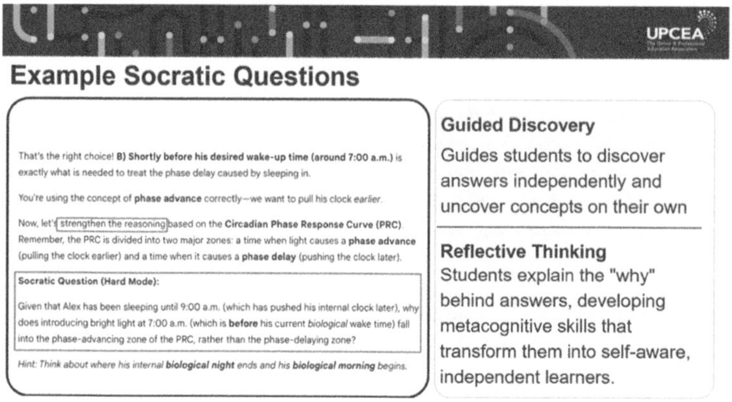

Figure 3.2 This AI model draws from course materials to pose Socratic style questions to students.

PB: The setup is pretty darn easy and we've done it for a new instructor for W26 in the MVS 340 course that I taught last term. Knowing that it worked for my course, he saw it and said that he would be interested in using it. So the material that he has for his students and my material is not 100% the same, so we basically created a new tutor based specifically on his material. All we needed to do was to put his slides into the Google folder. We then added his learning objectives into our system prompt, and that's basically all there is to this setup piece.

At that point the student can begin, and they're given a pre-assessment. The student then tells the system which learning objective they want to work on, and the tutor is able to give them a question for them to answer to get a sense of where their knowledge gaps may be.

And based on that pre-assessment, the system begins to jump in and is able to conduct some personalized learning. It begins to have a back and forth, and ask them some questions in order to see how they're doing.

And in this first phase it is all very straightforward. It's just pointing at the Google folder, that's these learning materials, and then the system prompt is where we put those learning objectives. And so, again, the course learning objectives are the only piece that's really added into our system prompt that is specific to the instructor. Some people think that we give the AI the questions, but actually, it is using the system prompt as well as the materials in order to develop those questions itself.

RB: And is this actually in use, or still in the pilot stage?

PB: So we used it in the classroom last term as a resource for students to help them prepare for their exam. And, with a couple small exceptions, it was not worth points toward the class…just a resource to help students prepare for the in-class exams.

In the pre-assessment once they provide an answer, the tutor is immediately following with an analysis of their answer and is able to kind of give some feedback.

So, it actually will go through and decide whether the student has met the objective or not, with a response at a level that it considers to be adequate, which is something we had to titrate over time.

Then we're able to kind of check the box, and this is kept in memory, so as they move forward, if there were 40 learning objectives for the exam, it's keeping track of the ones they've attempted, and which ones they had actually mastered, or, you know, getting the approval and which ones they're really off the mark, and which ones they're making progress on.

And then the personalized tutoring is pretty interesting. So, it works on a scaffold where, on the front end, it's doing some hand-holding if the student needs it. This is just natural language, so rather than for instance is the answer A, B, C, D, or E, they're typing in their response in order to show the tutor what they know or don't know.

RB: So, seeing this, it raises a couple of questions. The first one is this primarily a learning tool to replace or supplement, let's say traditional kinds of reading and discussions, or is this also designed to be an assessment tool in terms of replacing or assessing papers and assignments?

PB: Definitely not for papers, I would say, because it's really more a back and forth that is more conceptual than feedback on something like a writing prompt. So this being a physiology course, it's not critiquing or giving feedback on writing structure. It's a resource that allows them more time to engage with the course materials in a highly specific way that is focused on the learning objectives of the instructor.

RB: Theoretically at least this could also be something, I suppose, that a human teacher could do, but well humans don't scale, and they don't have the same ways of generating this amount of analytical information as this chat can do. Would that be the reason an individual teacher would choose an AI like this over doing the questioning themselves?

PB Yes, I would say scale would be my biggest reason, and my class is 80 students. I'm using most of my time in class to talk about the material, and to give them, at a whole class level, some practice with it, but the AI allows them to then individually go in and have immediate feedback on their understanding.

RB: So would you say this tool would be categorized as a test prep tool then?

PB: I would say that the students used it in this last term that way as an exam prep. Others that have seen it feel that it's also very useful to fill the gap of knowledge in students that are less well-prepared.

RB: Would a goal of this initiative be to reduce a certain percentage of a general AI? Because clearly it doesn't stop anyone from doing it if they choose to still use it of course.

PB: So I think it's a really different thing. In this case, this is not worth points, right? The use is intended to help them to bring their knowledge base up so that they can be successful, on exams, on summative exams.

And so, I think, this relates to the opposite of where a lot of people are thinking that somebody can just use ChatGPT to answer all the questions. In this case, we are kind of flipping the framing a bit, and saying, so ultimately, we want to see that you're capable of building your knowledge base of this material, and this is a tool that will help you to do that. It's using grounded principles of learning and retaining information.

RB: Is this tool applicable for writing and paper assignments?

PB: Well I'm talking about a course where 60% of the grade is coming from in-class exams, and so this is really helpful for preparation for those in-class exams. As it relates to writing prompts and assignments, that's a pretty different beast, and I don't anticipate that this tool is going to be helpful for that. So we're struggling with that piece.

On the matter of writing though, here at Michigan we have had a "writing to learn" program since before the pandemic through our Sweetland Writing Center. When Generative AI came along we realized that we needed to "reduce the benefit" of students simply entering our writing prompts to "produce" a paper. So we were trying to think about what is/are the detail(s) that we could leave out of our writing prompts, where we could refer students back to the course materials and say, something like you're going to need to refer back to what we covered in Unit 1 in order to properly answer this question, and in your writing product, you need to be referring back to that material in specific ways, and not to any other material. So, in other words if they just copy and paste the assignment into ChatGPT and copy and paste back the answer or the response, it's very likely to miss the mark. So we're reducing the benefit of that behavior by making sure they include important details that relate specifically to our course content.

RB: Though I guess, given how vast the amount of data that Gen AI systems are scooping up. I imagine you also want to make sure that your course materials are fully proprietary, and not just articles available on the open web, or even book chapters that students could sort of throw to the AI to scoop up.

PB: Yeah, so that's a great point, and certainly one can think, I can just grab all the lecture materials and throw them into it, as part of the broader prompt. So you're absolutely right. I think at this point the first semester students in our program are less likely to be that advanced in their thinking. But you're certainly right that this is something that could be done.

And we're always just trying to think about new strategies. A year ago, we had something that I think now is no longer difficult for generative AI to do, and it was working for us to reduce the benefit a year ago. There we just said after you finish your writing, go through and revisit the rubric, and then go through your writing, and highlight in blue where you have answered Rubric Part 2, and highlight in yellow where you've answered Rubric Part 3. And so on. So we think that this is another thing that GenAI is now pretty capable of doing automatically, but my point is that we just try to identify ways that we can reduce the benefit of students trying to use GenAI to… I'll use the word cheat in this case, to kind of shortcut their assignments.

RB: Back to the Wolverine project, have you tried to figure out how successful it was overall? Did you get student feedback?

PB: Yes, long after the grades were out, we sent a voluntary survey, and we got feedback from 24 of the 80-ish students in the class, a little better than 25%. And 91% of those 24 agreed that it was effective in identifying their areas of weakness and helping them to build expertise. So, we were really happy about that.

Also, 78% strongly agreed that it was effective at improving their understanding of the material, and in fact, we didn't have anybody who was neutral or disagreed, so basically 100% agreed, at some level, that it was helpful for them improving their understanding. And the majority of them, 79%, would be excited to have it for use in other courses, which is something we're working on now.

RB: One tough question I like to ask my interviewees in this whole matter is if you have tried or think there are any strategies that would motivate a student, on their own, to choose of their own volition to use AI when it is not appropriate or good for their learning.

PB: I recently had a conversation with someone here in the School of Information, and they had what I thought was a really interesting approach. So they're teaching the ability to write code and this instructor was basically having the students on the front end sign a kind of contract to say, here is what I intend to do with this course: here is what I think I need to get out of this course, and here's my intended use of Gen AI in this course. The idea was that the students could then identify whether it was actually important for them to know how to write Java code in the course—or whether they just needed to be able to get the code written. And could use GenAI to do it. To put it another way, the concept was that the students would be forward thinking to what kind of job they anticipated they were pursuing—and whether it appeared critical for them to be able to write code from scratch—or not.

And if so, then they, presumably, should really make minimal use of Gen AI. They would have an option to use it in very particular ways, but not just doing all the code writing for them.

In my view too, I think that being explicit about such things is important, because, even though I'm quite Gen AI-forward in regard to my own use of it and exposure of it to students, there are spaces where it just doesn't make sense.

Also it's important to talk about the incentives. The whole purpose of our classes should be about learning, not about the grade. I think in Canada and in the US students are just so ingrained to feel that the whole purpose of school is to get the grade, to get to the next step. And that's really become a very unfortunate thing in that we have trained all students to believe well, I can earn the grade by pasting in some information that I never read.

RB: Yeah, actually, under such an incentive structure, doing that is a perfectly logical approach to get from here to there if the only goal that you think you're expected to achieve is a good grade, right?

PB: Yep, there you go.

RB: Is there anything else we did not get a chance to discuss that you would like to add?

PB: Yes, just one other piece. I don't think it's radically new, but I also think it's a great opportunity, which is using this same RAG model, but instead of the system prompt being a Socratic tutor, using it to be more as an interactive case study. In fact we have been using it now as a virtual patient and a virtual client.

One of my colleagues has a sales class too, and so as I understand it, he has the system prompt set where you have to build rapport with the virtual client before you can make the ask for the sale. It's an attempt to build it to be a very real-world interaction that can then be evaluated and practiced 24-7. You don't need to hire an actor to play the role, you can use the chatbot to practice your pitch, or practice your bedside manner, or whatever the case might be.

Peter Bodary is a clinical associate professor of Applied Exercise Science and Movement Science and associate dean of undergraduate Education at the University of Michigan School of Kinesiology.

Ivo Visak, CEO, AI Leap Foundation, Tallinn, Estonia

> *The biggest value of a teacher nowadays is to be kind of an emotional coach...the worst-case scenario is "let's wait and see," because while you're waiting, all the students are using the versions that are a net negative educationally.*

AI Leap is an Estonian educational innovation program helping schools adapt to the age of AI and fostering meaningful learning through an app and related program initiatives. It has deployed a specialized, research-backed "Socratic model" AI app to high schoolers nationwide alongside comprehensive teacher training, aiming to programmatically elevate students' higher-order thinking and self-regulation skills rather than letting commercial chatbots dictate their learning habits. To track pedagogical impact, researchers are leveraging anonymized European data chunks and tool metadata to measure growth in student interaction alongside shifts in teaching practices, Ultimately, Visak stresses that while tireless LLMs are necessary to solve classroom scaling limitations, the technology forces a complete rejection of traditional, easily automated homework in favor of highly valued, face-to-face classroom time focused on human empathy and cognitive mentorship.

RB: So, I'd like to discuss the AI Leap Foundation and the app it created. Would you say that production and dissemination of the App is the primary function of the foundation?

IV: I would say it's one of the main functions of the foundation, because we have multiple functions. Quite a bit of Estonian researchers are involved with it, that are quite highly respected among Estonian teachers. We call it a Socratic model of AI.

As a foundation, we are very heavily investing into teacher training programs. Estonia's education system has been the number one country in PISA tests in Europe for the past five or six years. So, we take education quite seriously here, and it's almost like a national sport.

So one part is training the teachers, the second is the clear dissemination of AI literacy to both students and the parents, and the third part is the technological solution, which is a research project with University of Tartu researcher Professor Jaan Aru, who's a brain researcher here in Estonia, who is also doing quite a bit of research together with Stanford University and with University of Tartu here in Estonia.

RB: What grade range is the app geared for?

IV: In this initial pilot year [2026], it's fully dedicated to upper secondary education and this time just toward 10th and 11th grade students. So, this year, all Estonian high schools who are getting the training for free.

Estonia is the size of Maine, which is about 1.4 million people while we're, about 1.3 million or so. So, you can imagine that all the teachers in Maine are getting the training and applications for studying.

RB: So, what do the teachers get exactly?

IV. We have a cooperation project with both OpenAI and Google and right now everybody gets ChatGPT, and some of the schools are also getting Gemini. It's been created as a year-long deal and soon we will have another contract period. We didn't want to sign a long contract because things change so quickly.

RB: Have you gotten any reaction yet, either informally or through actual studies from the teachers or the students, to how it's met your goal and what you're hearing back in terms of how it's working?

IV: We have a pretty clear set of simple KPIs and wider measurements on how we measure success.

The simple ones are the numbers. Out of the 155 high schools we have in Estonia, 155 have joined the program. In Estonia, we have around 4,800 Estonian high school teachers, and we have given them all licenses, at minimum ChatGPT Plus licenses.

RB: Right. And in terms of the goals, have you done any digging deeper in terms of changes in the way studying or learning is being done? Reactions either informal, from students or teachers, or any actual rigorous studies, or is that still to come?

IV: So, we've now getting the initial information from the teachers. One of the key KPIs we are looking at right now is the effectiveness of the teacher's time usage. Around 1,200 teachers responded to that question, and 70.4% of the teachers have self-reported that they see that the use of AI has made certain elements of their work more useful. Another very important KPI for us is looking at the effect on teaching practices and methods. Currently, 52% have said that they have already changed their teaching practices. Our aim for the end of the school year is 70%, so we're not there yet.

One of the main aims of AI Leap is that the students have better learning skills, and we are aiming at improving it through self-regulation. This is something that we are going to do using testing methods with our partners at the University of Tartu. We're getting the data through students directly, but also through the research on how they use the tool, so we are also getting quite a bit of metadata from the tool usage.

RB: How do you actually measure usage? Is it looking at data from the actual system itself that you'll be examining? Are there any privacy issues here?

IV: That is some part of it. We will preserve people's privacy, but you have to research new technology on both positive and negative effects.

Through our partnership with OpenAI and Google, the data is here in Europe, and through anonymization, we can create very big chunks of data and look at the automated data in a very direct way. What we look for is there a learning skill, or growth in the interaction with the tools?

RB: Is this application utilized only in the classroom? Does it prevent students from just going to the normal, typical ChatGPT once again at home?

IV: At the end of the day, we can't control what they use at home, but when we did a pilot with ten high schools, we found that a larger percentage of students enjoyed using our application more than general AI because they trusted it more. It works pretty well in not breaking from the tasks it has been given on the learning skills side. Students showcased said they were much happier and that the teachers are more okay with this kind of tool supported by Estonian researchers.

RB: One educator, Clay Shirky, a provost for learning at NYU, wrote an op-ed saying that it didn't matter what he told the faculty, the students just used AI whenever and however they wanted. He eventually concluded that the only way to truly assess how a student is doing is to go back and do those same Socratic discussions and oral methods, but it has to be in the physical place. You give the test there—oral discussion, no computers, no Internet. You might even have to use the old-fashioned "Blue Books." What's your reaction to this approach?

IV: This "blue book" thing might not be bad. A lot of the old teaching methods are good teaching methods. I mostly sign on to the idea, but there's an asterisk to it. We have to value the time we spend together with the students more. Out of all of this crazy stuff that's happening in the world, it's one of those great moments where the education systems are looking into the mirror and really asking what is really important. Because in all of the hours afterward, we have less control.

This brings me to the whole concept of homework. I think there are very few homework assignments that make sense anymore. Most of the ways we have been giving homework here in Estonia are completely pointless. There is very little homework, at least in some schools I know in Finland, Germany, and the Netherlands. Their philosophy has already changed so that it all comes down to what is healthy for a student. Is overworking students healthy? If teachers don't understand that the education system is not the same, then maybe it would be a good idea to start thinking about another career.

RB: When I was speaking to someone who created their own custom question asking chatbot for their classroom… I asked them, "Is there any reason why these questions couldn't be asked by the teacher?"

IV: The problem in an educational environment is scale. In Estonia, 99% of education is public education. From the perspective of the teacher, it's almost humanly impossible if you have, let's say, 36 students in a classroom [the maximum permitted in Estonian classrooms] to give the same attention to everyone. LLMs don't get tired of explaining a narrative to you. They will never get tired of explaining something to you, and they will always have time for you.

RB: But what happens to the subtle knowledge that only a teacher could know about the student? For example, one teacher told me something that stuck in my mind was that unlike a human teacher, AI can't mimic, say knowing that Johnny's father was arrested yesterday, or that Janet's parents are going through a divorce, and so on, which will change how that teacher interacts and perhaps even instructs them.

IV: True. There are very clear borders of what LLM is capable of. It's a mimicking device. It won't have, at least in its current form, human brain chemistry, and the empathy that another human being has toward another is something else.

But at the same time, the mimicking effect is something which some people are craving, because maybe for the first time in their life, suddenly there's a tool that talks really nicely to them.

RB: Any final thoughts?

IV: My main worry is that we are not dealing with all this. The worst-case scenario is "let's wait and see," because while you're waiting, all the students are using the versions that are a net negative educationally. You have to have an idea as a society that we can't allow these things to just run on their own course. We have to help the teachers and students, and discuss with these tech partners that these tools can be useful, but to listen to us as educators. I wrote an article along these lines last November, titled *Doing nothing is not a strategy,* that also conceptualizes our way of doing things a bit.

There is also something going on now that is akin to a Trojan horse effect. Most Western education systems have never been in a situation where they have had a mirror so much in front of them. What is an education system in an age where there are tools that mostly answer everything? What is the role of the teacher? Teachers can never really cross the gap between information and knowledge anymore. The biggest value of a teacher nowadays is to be kind of an emotional coach.

RB: Right, it's causing everybody to rethink things. If it was a newspaper headline, it could be AI may be saving education, but not in the way you think.

IV: That's a pretty good summary. AI is forcing people to get out of their comfort zone.

Ivo Visak is the CEO of the AI Leap Foundation (TI-Hüpe) and leads Estonia's national initiative to integrate AI-based learning tools into secondary and vocational education with a focus on responsible, human-centered adoption of new technologies.

Contact: ivo@tihupe.ee

4 When No One Is Watching

Motivating Students to Resist the Cognitive Shortcut

Chapters 2 and 3 profiled educators who created a variety of "top down" classroom design strategies to address their concerns over potential harms to their students' learning and critical thinking from cognitive offloading to AI. Those professors intentionally created new forms of assignments and assessments geared to steer students away from inappropriate use of AI, or in some cases, introduced more educationally sound AI models.

The top down classroom design approach can be highly effective and, in fact, is the preferred method for controlling or guiding appropriate student use of AI. But one vexing challenge remains: what happens when the student is in a location other than the classroom: a library, café, dorm, and so on? Even the best classroom practices-whether they are AI-resistant ones or systems that integrate Socratic AI questioning trained on class material—still have one significant limitation: it is virtually impossible to monitor or detect unauthorized/detrimental AI usage when the student is back home or in other unsupervised locations. If the student still decides to use ChatGPT, Gemini, Claude, or any public AI to substitute for their own thinking and learning struggles, an educator's carefully constructed system to control their students' usage of AI could be diluted or even nullified.

Some students are quite aware of the risks AI's seductive allure can have on their education. In the April 10, 2026 issue of *The Atlantic* on AI and learning, the reporter shared the concerns of one student, who said he was "grateful that he finished high school when he did…If the latest AI tools had been around then… he might have been tempted to use them to do his homework". [The student], now a sophomore at Stanford, finished high school all the way back in 2024. "I have a younger sibling who is just graduating high school," he said. "Our educational experience has been vastly different, even though we're just two years apart" (Shroff, 2026).

An "Unfair Position"

Some educators may consider students who use AI when not authorized to do so, simply as cheaters. And while that perspective is understandable, and not

DOI: 10.4324/9781003770978-5

without *any* merit, it's also worth considering the position AI has put students in, which Stanford University Professor of Graduate Education Susanna Loeb and Faculty Director, SCALE Initiative (SCALE describes what it does is "conducts rigorous research, identifies, supports and scales promising solutions and engages decision-makers to integrate research, policy, and practice across critical issues in K-12 education") simply calls *unfair*. "It is nearly impossible to overcome the ease with which you can produce something using an LLM. It is our responsibility as teachers not to put them in that position."

And it is true that we are all biased to moving toward the immediate rewards in front of us versus some uncertain and vague future benefits. And given a certain goal, we normally choose the path of least resistance. M. Scott Peck, author of the 1970s best seller, *The Road Less Traveled*, has called this human tendency a natural form of laziness and even a kind of "original sin," as we all are afflicted with it. We also know that the fastest and easiest route is so often not the wisest choice.

And certainly, if the will and wisdom to defer gratification is hard for adults, it is even harder for children and young adults who are not yet fully mature.

Consider the traditional paramount goals and incentives made clear in most classrooms: a high grade, and getting an assignment completed on time. These motivations easily lead students to relieve that pressure and meet those goals by tapping one's keyboard to summon AI.

So how can educators play a role in helping students make better AI use choices when they are on their own? Given both human and classroom motivational constraints, this is admittedly quite a challenge. And while it is unlikely that this problem can ever be completely resolved, there are potential remedies.

This chapter will describe several such approaches. As with the strategies shared in Chapter 3, educators should consider which strategies are most likely to be relevant and effective, based on their own set of circumstances, for example, students' level; subject; class size; teaching style; and other contextual factors.

However, before discussing the methods to steer students to making wiser and more appropriate AI usage decisions, it is important to first examine the most fundamental matter, students understanding of *learning* itself.

First Things First: Knowing and Caring about Learning

Educators know that students believe certain things that happen in the classroom as important to them: grades, deadlines, assignments, the teacher, and even—hopefully—the subject matter. But they generally don't think about learning itself or why it matters.

Why not? Dr. Mary English, Senior Associate Director, Center for Advancing Teaching and Learning Through Research (CATLR) at Northeastern University in Boston, MA offers one key reason: many students today view education transactionally—that is, you go to college to get a job; to get a job you get a degree; and to get a good degree, you need to get A grades. The learning, then, gets lost in the focus on productivity. She also adds that students often take four and five disparate classes and are overloaded with reading assignments that often have no clear connection to core learning objectives nor to each other. So, without clear purpose or applicability classes can all feel irrelevant. And the students' concentration in college often tends to be on getting those A's and moving on.

While the primary focus of this chapter is how to create strategies to motivate students to go well beyond engaging in that hollow transaction, English cautions that while the right motivations are critical, "unless students know the difference between productivity and learning, and why learning is important, the motivation may never be activated."

It's worth digging deeper. In her book, *Creating Self-Regulated Learners* (Routledge, 2013), Linda Nilson unpacks the problematic relationship between students and learning like this:

- Students may think of themselves as students rather than learners (citing Weimer, 2012)
- Most students don't think about how they learn; they may struggle to produce any insights into their own learning (citing Weimer, 2014)
- They may think learning should be easy, rather than hard and effortful, because it has been easy in their past schooling.

Nilson suggests that educators can help students become more aware of their own learning by engaging in a substantive back-and-forth discussion on the topic (which probably is best done in the first or second class session). She advises that during the discussion, the always important "why" and the "so what" questions should be addressed. (English adds that these questions should also be addressed throughout; students should know the why, so what, and context for everything they're doing.) The Transparent Assignment Design framework (making learning processes more explicit for students) explains this as does applying backward planning/design and instructional/constructive alignment. These help focus on the materials and assignments so that the connections to core learning objectives become clearer for both instructor and students.

Nilson also recommends priming the discussion about learning by assigning students some reading. One is *Learning (Your First Job)* written in 2002 by Robert Leamnson (https://www1.udel.edu/CIS/106/iaydin/07F/misc/first Job.pdf). The 12-page essay discusses in an informal but compelling manner why the very *first* job of a college student is to know how to learn.

Another Key Piece of the Puzzle: Helping Students *Monitor* Their Own Learning

A key strategy educators should seriously consider as part of the learning process is to help students become *Self-Regulated Learners.*

What Is *Self-Regulated* Learning?

While you may be familiar with the benefits that accrue to students who apply meta-awareness during their learning, you are probably less aware of self-regulated learning (SRL), a formal model first introduced by educator Barry Zimmerman in the 1990s (Schunk & Zimmerman, 1994).

Self-Regulated Learners have the ability to apply metacognitive, emotional, and physical strategies to monitor and regulate their learning process. Nilson fleshes out the definition as "the conscious planning, monitoring, evaluation, and ultimately control of one's learning in order to maximize it … It means being mindful, intentional, reflective, introspective, self-aware, self-controlled, and self-disciplined about learning, and it leads to becoming self-directed." (Nilson, 2014). https://www.facultyfocus.com/articles/teaching-and-learning/secret-self-regulated-learning/

There is clear evidence in the educational literature that the key elements of SRL work: in fact, not only has it been shown to have a positive impact on a student's learning but shown to have a *large* impact (Hattie, 2009).

There are actually three phases that a self-regulated learner engages in during their learning activity:

(1) At the Start of the Activity. At the very beginning, a self-regulated learner engages in careful planning; identifying their goals, how they will approach achieving those goals, and developing an initial plan of action.

(2) During the Learning Activity. While engaged in their research, analysis, or specific learning activity, the self-regulated learner continually monitors what they are learning. They note if any materials or processes are confusing, and identify hurdles blocking the path toward their goals. When they notice these obstacles or setbacks, they make whatever adjustments that seem necessary and reasonable (e.g., slowing down to absorb more difficult materials, reexamining the means taken to achieve the goals, and reaffirming or adjusting the appropriateness of their goals)

In essence, they are watching themselves learn and assessing how it is going while they are engaged in the process.

(3) When the Learning Activity is Completed. After the project is completed, a self-regulated learner reflects on how their learning went, if they achieved their goals, if not why, and think about what they should do next.

How Common Are Self-Regulated Learners and How Are Skills Developed?

Research indicates that while students' SRL abilities exist on a low-to-high spectrum most students are not high self-regulated learners. For those that are high in SRL, researchers have discovered that those skills were initially developed by observing others who are have the skill and model the processes. But in order to fully develop and build SRL capacities, they need to actually engage in learning activities themselves and apply them.

Can SRL Skills Be Taught?

As the majority of students in a classroom are not high-level self-regulated learners, it raises a key question: can educators do anything to teach students how to be mindful and regulate their learning processes?

Fortunately, the answer is yes.

In their 2013 article, *Supporting Student Self-Regulated Learning in Problem- and Project-Based Learning* (English & Kitsantas, 2013), the authors examined the development of SRL (in the context of using a Project-Based Learning pedagogy). They found that the teacher can create learning environments that support students' development of their skills, and do so during the following key phases:

During Phase 1 (Project/Problem Launch), at the start of the assignment, the instructor provides a well-crafted *driving* question (an open-ended, real-world query that serves as a catalyst for student investigation) or a problem that provides an appropriate amount of structure with clearly stated learning goals, launcher activities, and activity structures. These approaches support the SRL skills of goal setting, strategic planning, and self-motivation.

During Phase 2 (Inquiry and Product/Solution Creation), the instructor can support the SRL skills of self-control and self-observation by employing techniques that make students' thinking visible, such as whiteboarding, formative assessments, journaling, and prompts for explanation. Further, the teacher should interact with students in the role of guide, encouraging help-seeking, prompting reflection and revision, and providing instructional support as needed in response to specific knowledge gaps identified through observations and formative assessments.

During Phase 3 (Conclusion), presentations, role plays, poster sessions, pin-up sessions, and gallery walks can facilitate reflection. The project/problem conclusion provides an opportunity for students to engage in thinking about their learning outcomes in relation to their goals, to identify the strategies and resources that worked well and those that didn't, and to determine what questions they still have. This practice lays the groundwork for students' development of this important intellectual habit, and should not be skipped or minimized.

Provide Wrappers with Assignments

Another approach that an educator can take to facilitate SRL, known by many in the SRL community, is by creating "wrappers" to accompany an assignment. Originally introduced by Marsha Lovett (Lovett, 2008), Vice Provost for Teaching and Learning Innovation and Professor of Psychology at Carnegie Mellon University, wrappers are supplementary instructional materials created by the educator and provided to the student upon being given an assignment. The wrapper, through guiding questions related to the assignment, instructs students *how* to perform the metacognitive steps and engage in reflections. These instructions are designed to be reviewed by the student before, during, and after the assignment. Wrappers can also accompany exams, where the process often starts when a graded exam is returned to students (the "after" phase) and then continues before the next exam to support students in enhancing their study strategies.

Nilson further describes wrappers as follows:

> *[Wrappers'] purpose is to heighten students' conscious awareness of their learning process: what they are and are not understanding or retaining, how they are or are not learning, what they are deeming important, how they are tackling and proceeding with an assignment, how they are processing and responding to a learning experience, how well they are executing and realizing their plans and goals, what value they are obtaining from a learning task, how much they are progressing on a given skill, how much confidence they have in their knowledge and skills, how much they may be overestimating their knowledge and skills, and how effectively and diligently they are preparing for quizzes and exams.*
>
> (Nilson, 2013, p. 13)

Nilson also explains that wrappers actually perform a double duty: they not only help students apply SRL skills to an assignment, but, at the same time, teach them how their mind works and how to make it learn and perform better. In doing so, wrappers "multiply the learning value of every standard class activity and assignment" (Nilson, 2013).

There are several explanations as to why, intuitively, wrappers can work so well to impart critical meta-level thinking skills. In a presentation made at Carnegie Mellon University in 2008, Lovett (2008) cited these reasons:

- They are time efficient (students and faculty will use them)
- Students are doing the task anyway

- A wrapper only adds a few minutes of time
- The metacognition practice is integrated with the task
- Students are self-monitoring in the context where it is needed
- Feedback on accuracy can be built in
- Wrapper support can be gradually faded (i.e., it can include fewer reflections as students complete subsequent wrappers across a course)

In addition to these more self-evident reasons, evidence-based research has also shown that wrappers support metacognitive awareness and promote SRL (you have to cite some of the research). For example, Lovett (2013) implemented exam wrappers across four introductory science courses, such that first-year college students experienced the intervention in one to three courses. In general, students' wrapper submissions indicated increased metacognitive awareness and use of more evidence-based learning strategies. Moreover, these positive changes increased as a function of students' number of wrapper courses, thus demonstrating a "dose-response" effect.

Wrappers offer additional benefits. For one they can supplement or enhance the assessment and grading process. And faculty can create them relatively easily without changing the way they teach or organize their class. This easiness overcomes perhaps the biggest objections educators raise when asked to implement recommended new teaching practices: finding the time to do so.

In a conversation I had with Lovett, she shared a few additional tips too on how to make wrappers as useful as possible. To help ensure that the student takes the necessary time and attention to complete them, the educator should provide some kind of incentive or intrinsic reward. This could be directly assessment-related, additional points for completing it thoughtfully, as well as softer but still significant rewards. For example, the educator can inform the student that the reflection piece will have value to remind them of something they might forget when it comes to study for the next exam and let them know that if they did not perform the way they wanted on one assignment, their analysis and reflection are designed to help them do better the next time. This way they don't see this as busy work but something to enhance their performance going forward.

Lovett also said that some faculty members she worked with, who held TA-led weekly discussions, would use one of these sessions to discuss the wrappers. Students could then share with each other what they found worked and did not work for their learning.

Finally, while adding wrappers is an easy lift for most professors since it does not change anything fundamental about creating the assignment, it can be made even easier if a professor can work off and tweak a template. This could be something created by an institution's Teaching and Learning center (and sample wrappers, categorized by subject can be found here: https://www.cmu.edu/teaching/designteach/teach/examwrappers/)

Note that wrappers also make the learner more conscious and deliberative in detecting when their use of AI is advancing or detracting from their learning goals. Lovett says, for instance that AI-use-related reflections can be added to a wrapper and include questions like: how ready was I to do this on my own given the way I used or didn't use AI, and then when I was tested in a situation where I couldn't use AI?

Finally, it's worth pointing out that research shows even minor interventions that frame a task in a new way (in this case, adding a wrapper to an assignment) can significantly create positive changes in a range of other learning behaviors.

Adjusting the Cost-Benefit Calculations for Using AI

As with most human decisions, when students decide that they will turn to AI during an assignment, they make a quick cost-benefit decision. And if they have a transactional mindset as to why they are in school, and the assignment they are working on does not spark their excitement or even much interest, and the deadline is near, their decision to use AI can certainly be considered a rational (though still likely a misguided and questionable) decision.

This is discouraging and a real challenge. And even the most skilled educators are not likely, within the scope of a single course, to change the mindset of a student who has a transactional approach for why they are in school. But there is an opportunity to produce the kind of assignments that provide motivation that can counter and even override the benefits of using AI, significantly changing its costs and benefits.

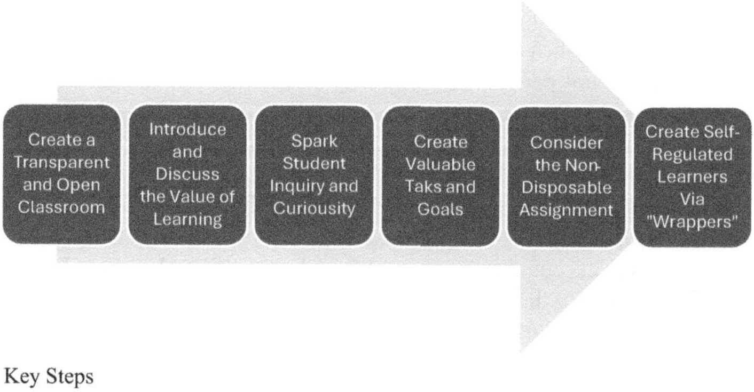

Figure 4.1 Key steps for motivating students to learn and engage.

Motivations

Although a discussion of the psychological motivational theories of learning is well beyond the scope of this book, famed educational researcher Paul Pintrich has determined the following as the three primary factors that motivate a student's desire to learn:

1. **Self-efficacy** (judgement that one is capable of doing the task assigned)
2. **Task value** (belief about the importance of interest in, and value of the task at hand)
3. **Goal orientation** (A motivating goal can include the mastery of a skill; a high grade or other extrinsic reasons, or an outcome that has a positive social impact on that student's achievement or standing in relation to other students)

Consider these motivators in the context of the AI cost/benefit decision. If a student is given an assignment and is bored and unengaged (low task value); and is only there for a grade (goal orientation), and there is a looming deadline, the benefits of a fast, convenient, and "good enough" AI are alluring. Add if the student has low self-efficacy, and is not confident they can even do a good job, AI looks even more attractive.

But an educator (or an educational institution) retains the option and ability to adjust student motivating levers to turn them from "just get this done as fast as possible" to "I'm psyched to learn on this topic." And, adds English, to structure the assignments and the course to place the emphasis on learning over grades.

In practice this means doing the following:

1. Engaging students by sparking their curiosity
2. Making the assignment tasks more meaningful
3. Creating more valuable end goal so the student will want to do as good a job as possible and is excited about the expected results of their work.

Creating the Right Classroom Environment

There is one foundational step to attend to before implementing these motivating strategies: producing a classroom atmosphere built on honesty, respect, and transparency. This is important for several reasons, but will be particularly important when it comes to developing any informal or formal AI usage agreements (discussed further).

There are of course myriad ways to create such a classroom; but one highly relevant strategy is to engage the class in an open discussion on developing one's own philosophy and ethical standing about AI. Just as individuals arrive at their own ethical stand on a range of contentious social issues, eating meat, using renewable energy, how to treat undocumented immigrants, and so on, we can all arrive at a personal philosophy and perspective on AI.

Such a conversation does double duty: it not only helps facilitate that honest and trusted classroom, but also helps students decide for themselves under what circumstance they personally feel it is appropriate or not appropriate to use the technology.

A good way to get the ball rolling is by the educator sharing their own philosophy and approach to the technology, including when and why they choose to use or not use AI, and for what reasons. Then, with the assurance of no judgment, and no right or wrong answers, students are prompted to share how they feel about AI: what do they know about it, what they like and don't like, and when and why they personally don't want to use it. If the educator can help students think deeply about their values, how AI fits in, and articulate a clear personal philosophy, they will have produced a well thought out philosophy to guide them to remain true to their own integrity.

[Note on May 25, 2026, Pope Leo XIV released his first Encyclical, *Magnifica humanitas: On Safeguarding the Human Person in the Time of Artificial Intelligence*. Of special note here is the fourth chapter, *Safeguarding Humanity at a Time of Transformation. Truth, Work, Freedom* (parag 140)

> *Educating people about the use of AI, then, involves teaching them to decide when and for what purpose it ought not to be used. The speed and ease with which answers or summaries can be obtained risk extinguishing the desire to ask questions, which is a process that bears fruit only over time. As Plato wrote, the deepest and most important things are learned only after much time and effort, by engaging in discussion with others, "striking upon" ideas and experiences together like flint until the spark of understanding is kindled within us. We must learn, then, how to exercise restraint in the use of AI and to protect our young people from the promise of the perfect machine, from that subtle temptation which renders human thought seemingly superfluous precisely when it is most needed.*
>
> Pope Leo XIV (2026)

Motivating Levers

But how to neutralize students' educational motivational lever set to "complete this transaction?" Educators can add three powerful levers to help move students more to wanting to build skills, and think and learn to compete with their transactional one.

As noted above these levers can be set so that they serve to:

1. *Engage* students by sparking their curiosity
2. Make the assignment *task* more meaningful

3 Produce a *goal* more valuable so the student wants to do as good a job as possible. This can be to develop the skills they need professionally, or even how it may be utilized by others, see more details in the discussion on "non-disposable assignments."

Engaging Students

Starting with the first level: how to engage students by sparking their curiosity and making their learning meaningful, relevant, and potentially even joyful. One form of pedagogy shown to be highly successful in engaging and exciting students is Inquiry-Based Learning (IBL).

Beth Archer-Kuhn is a Professor with the Faculty of Social Work at the University of Calgary and co-author of *Reigniting Curiosity and Inquiry in Higher Education: A Realist's Guide to Getting Started with Inquiry-Based Learning.* She also has co-written a guide, titled *Inquiry Based Learning: A Guide for Social Work Educators in Higher Education.* In that guide Archer-Kuhn describes IBL as follows:

> *IBL is a "self-directed, question driven, search for understanding" can help students systematically move to a higher level of understanding. It happens in an environment where students are engaged in essentially open ended, learner-centered, hands on activities .... Inquiry-based learning (IBL) facilitates active and deep learning, affording a student the opportunity to explore and develop central questions about a particular subject through exploration. The purpose of inquiry is to "develop the skills needed to bring research to bear on the understanding of a central question" (Hudspith &a; Jenkins, 2007 p. 10). To this end, IBL is a process about discovery and systematically moving from one level of understanding to another, higher level.*
>
> (Archer-Kuhn, 2020)

The heart of inquiry, of course, is curiosity and asking questions. In his final book, *Building a Bridge to the 18th Century* (Postman 1999), Neil Postman wrote "question-asking is the most significant intellectual tool human beings have." He expands that point by adding:

> "What will happen if a student, studying history, asks, Whose history is this?... What will happen if a student, being given a set of facts, asks, What is a fact? How is it different from an opinion? And who is the judge?"

What about curiosity-do we all have it and can it be taught? In an interview, Archer-Kuhn said all children are, in fact, born curious; however, that natural curiosity and question asking activities too often get discouraged at home or during school years. So, by the time they enter higher education or even secondary school, they don't think anyone really wants to hear their ideas. Furthermore, given the recent fraught political times, students may hold back from talking, feeling certain questions and statements are not "safe."

To help students practice learning that it is OK to ask questions (and okay not to be right), consider the "structured controversy" Archer-Kuhn created where students address a contentious issue and then create arguments based specifically on what they heard the other student say.

[This is reminiscent of the listening advice from Neil Postman, in his *Teaching as a Subversive Activity* (1969), where he recommends using a technique pioneered by Psychologist Carl Rogers in his 1961 classic treatise *On Becoming a Person: A Therapist's View of Psychotherapy:*

> *In this article Rogers describes a particularly effective technique for teaching listening: the students engage in a discussion of some issue about which they have strong feelings. But their discussion has an unusual rule applied to it. A student may say anything he wishes but only after he has restated what the previous speaker has said to that speaker's satisfaction. Astounding things happen to students when they go through this experience. They find themselves concentrating on what others are saying to the point, sometimes, of forgetting what they themselves were going to say. In some cases, students have a unique experience. They find that they have projected themselves into the frame of mind of another person.*]
>
> (Postman, 1969)]

In Archer-Kuhn's Inquiry *Based Learning Guide* she provides worksheets and exercises for educators on how to develop and lead students through these kinds of productive question asking activities (see: https://bit.ly/4vftEDk).

Each educator based on their class subject, student level, and so on will naturally need to make their own determinations as to what types of curiosity engaging assignments work. To come up with these, teachers might query their students directly as to what aspect of the course they are most interested in learning about and discovering (within reasonable scope and boundaries). If the class is small, this could be accomplished through one-on-one discussions and for larger classes as a survey.

Note that IBL is not, of course, the only teaching method that can empower students to get excited about learning. There are other learner-centered teaching philosophies with the same goal of awakening student desire to learn. These include experiential learning such as project-based learning (PBL) and a still lesser known model called heutagogy.

In a discussion with Nazreen Beaulieu, Educational Technology and Instructional Design Specialist at the University of Saskatchewan Library, she states that she relies on heutagogy as a metacognitive approach to learning that she and her colleagues emphasize to help students make informed decisions about their use of AI and avoid offloading their thinking when doing so would be detrimental to their learning. She explained heutagogy as

> *a form of self-determined learning that emphasizes double-loop reflection and helps students develop their own agency in the learning process. It follows a constructivist approach that permits learners to construct knowledge for themselves while actively engaging in critical and reflective thinking. With the use of learning inventories, we meet students where they are, and make sure we build reflective practice into the process. We ask them to reflect on questions like "are you learning more or less with AI for certain tasks? How is the use of AI affecting you or your confidence? How might AI be detrimental to your learning if you don't do the actual work?"*

She added that

> *Heutagogy, learner agency, and critical thinking intersect in meaningful and mutually reinforcing ways. Heutagogy provides the learning approach that centers control with the learner; learner agency is the capacity that enables students to make choices within that space; and critical thinking is the skillset that allows those choices to be thoughtful, reflective, and informed. Together, they support learners in not only directing their own learning, but in evaluating, questioning, and adjusting how they engage with tools like AI.*

What about games to spur curiosity and learning? There is of course an enormous amount of literature and case studies on how to engage students through gamification, and it is too large a topic to cover here. Suffice it to say that while games alone cannot enhance or motivate learning on their own, if carefully designed to cultivate learning, they can be a good supplement to other techniques.

There are also methods that can motivate students to learn by making the assignment tasks more meaningful and the goal more valuable: designing a "non-disposable assignment."

Disposing of the Disposable Assignment

The vast majority of student papers and projects can, sadly, be categorized as "disposable assignments": that is, after the student's work is turned in, reviewed, and graded, they are likely discarded. But in stark contrast, "non-disposable" assignments are designed from the ground up to have an authentic and practical life and value *outside* of the classroom. These are intentionally designed upfront by the educator along with the student (or team of students, or as a full class).

There are levels of these more authentic non-disposable assignments which can range from producing readings or resources for future classes, to projects made publicly available, say a strategic plan for a non-profit organization or a market research report for a company as part of an experiential course project. Others can even be published as an open educational resource (OER), available and of potential value to the larger community.

Assignments made available to a wider public require more upfront planning, care, and attention than the other authentic projects that remain inside the institution. But they do not need to be overly complex or necessarily created as formal scholarly work; they could, for instance, take the form of podcasts, digital newsletters, YouTube videos, and online tutorials.

Another non-disposable assignment would be to have students create posters to present their work, mimicking a conference poster session, open to anyone inside and outside the educational institutions. (This assignment is also valuable, at least for grad students, to provide a practice run for creating future posters for conferences in their discipline.)

Finally, a fully licensed open source *renewable* work will need to adhere to more specific external procedures of OER publishing conventions and specifications. But these can also offer the greatest rewards—the highest task and goal motivators—by providing the student with the personal accomplishment of working toward having their (very likely first) work published, with their name publicly listed as author, admiration from family and friends, and a practical resume/portfolio artifact for future career purposes.

As one testament to the high level of motivation and rewards that renewable assignments can offer, how often (ever?) have you heard a student say that they were "thrilled" by the outcome of their assignment? That's the feeling though, that Robin DeRosa, the Executive Director of the Open Education Network, reported some of her students felt when seeing their names on a published open access work. English adds to that the same kind of excitement that students have reported feeling when they work with external project sponsors, receive feedback, and know that the work they did is serving a purpose.

I had the chance to have an email-based discussion with DeRosa about renewable assignments and the role the Open Education Network plays in helping faculty and students facilitate these projects. (The Open Network is an organization whose mission is to empower faculty, remove barriers to learning and knowledge-sharing, and enhance student success.)

DeRosa emphasized to me that these kinds of assignments are most effective when a course topic intersects meaningfully with the outside world, allowing students to contribute to a broader public conversation.

She also warns that a foundational rule of successful open pedagogy is that a faculty member must never unilaterally force a student's work to be public. Instead, the process must serve as a vehicle for student agency, where learners are explicitly taught the benefits, copyright structures, and potential risks of open licensing so they can choose their own paths. She also highlights that non-disposable work is not limited to traditional scholarly publishing; it can actually span a diverse range of formats—including podcasts, YouTube videos, blogs, and open-source data contributions—and can be effectively applied across all educational tiers, including vocational and trades education.

Regarding its use in vocational and trades, DeRosa recommended two excellent sources that tackle this issue. One is the Open Source book *Open Pedagogy in the Trades: Instructor Resource* by Bruce Neid and Nicki Rehn and available at: https://opentextbc.ca/tradesopenpedagogy/. And the other is the work of Chad Flinn, Electrical and Entrepreneurship Instructor at British Columbia Institute of Technology (BCIT) Burnaby, BC—see his "Open Pedagogy in Trades Education video" here: https://rethinkld.trubox.ca/chapter/open-pedagogy-in-trades-education/

Finally, for faculty who want to try this approach and wants help, she directs educators to collaborative infrastructure networks like her own Open Education Network (OEN) and university librarians, who can provide the necessary publishing tools and peer support. Ultimately, she argues that moving away from disposable assignments revitalizes under-supported faculty by transforming students from passive consumers into active, energized contributors to their fields and communities.

Non-Disposable Assignments Impact on AI Usage

Yet another advantage of the non-disposable assignment is that it can serve as one more motivator to *not* use AI in a harmful manner, as students can be informed by their instructor that they may need to explain and answer questions about their work to a public audience.

These motivators can be discussed in class, and reinforced again by adding these into the assignment wrapper. The following are examples of both positive and negative reinforcing motivators that can be told by the educator to their students.

Positive Reinforcement:

This is an opportunity to display your authentic voice to a larger public. Think of this as your first professionally displayed work and you want to make sure that it represents your own thinking and voice. That means it may not be perfect, but will reflect to others who you are, what you think, feel is important and needs attention and discussion outside of the classroom.

Negative Reinforcement:

You may get questions about your work and findings from another teacher, student, or someone knowledgeable outside of our school. If you relied on AI and it made an error you did not detect, and you are asked to defend it and don't know how to do so, it can create an uncomfortable situation. And even if a piece of AI-generated content is accurate, but you can't speak to it and expand how it was located, it can raise questions as to why you are unable to do so.

Creating a Pledge

Finally, as another motivator educators can create a reinforcing pledge, where each student, as part of their work, adds an AI usage statement. For example, if AI was not permitted at all, a statement could read:

This research and presentation were conducted and authored entirely by the [student(s) names]. No generative AI was used in the conceptualization, data analysis, or drafting of this work (signature).

OR if the student did get permission to use AI in some approved narrower ways (for instance to summarize a large set of data; or for grammar review or to produce an image, etc.), you can tell students that this could be fine and in fact, it has become increasingly commonly accepted practice by scholars, as long as they are fully transparent about any use of AI, and how to state it. Here is an example of a statement:

AI was utilized in this project for certain data summarization and grammar check applications. All of *the conceptualization, data analysis, and drafting of this work were done exclusively by (name and signature)*

This latter situation where AI can be acceptable under agreed upon narrow circumstance also provides an opportunity for a discussion between the educator and the student to come up with a jointly agreed upon determination on when in fact AI should be permitted (after arriving at some meaningful criteria: for example, does use of AI for doing X interfere with this class's core learning goals, etc.) but is not permitted for Y as it can impede thinking, learning, and skill development?

Other reasons these agreements on the proper use of AI are valuable is that it addresses one of the primary areas of confusion and distress by students today: missing, inconsistent, or contradictory policies on AI use; and it reinforces understanding of what learning really is.

This pledge, or integrity contract, can also work in two ways: the educator may agree what is appropriate and acceptable for their *own* AI use in the classroom. As noted in Chapter 1, it's not just that educators don't like students using AI, but students don't like to find that their professors are doing it either. So, an agreed upon pledge could include both students and the educator adhering to an agreement as to when it is and is not acceptable to use AI.

Of course, like any agreement based on trust and good will (sometimes called a "relational contract"), there is no real way to monitor, let alone enforce compliance. (For a discussion on best practices on how to make these types of agreements most effective, see *Building Classroom Trust with Technology: Create an Honor Contract to Support Academic Honesty*, published online in November 2025 by the University of Chicago.) See in particular the section that recommends a strategy created by David A. Rettinger and Tricia Bertram Gallant where the honor contract can be reinforced via gentle "nudges" throughout the course. (From their work: *The Opposite of Cheating: Teaching for Integrity in the Age of AI.*)

Other Informal Motivators

This chapter examines the accepted evidence based on psychological and learning motivators that can help students, when on their own, make choices to use or not use AI that are more healthy, appropriate, and are aligned to skill building, learning, and maintaining their own integrity.

There are also positive and negative standalone non-AI usage reinforcement strategies that can be shared with students, listed below. These have been drawn from surveys of students and more informal reports on why some students have, on their own, chosen to avoid AI use or are very skeptical about the technology. They are grouped into two categories: Negative Reinforcement Motivators and Positive Reinforcement Motivators. For each, there is a suggested method for highlighting this concern to a student.

Negative Reinforcement Strategies

Anti-GenAI Usage Motivator	*Motivational Strategy*
I may become too dependent on AI for my thinking	1. Show images of brain neuron activity weakening during AI uses 2. Create future scenarios where thinking is degraded
I will no longer be able to retain information as well	1. Explain how we encode our memory and recall methods 2. Create future scenarios where memory is not as robust
If my unauthorized use of AI is detected, there will be negative consequences I will suffer	1. Explain to students that you will see indicators that suggest their work has been used by AI, and if it does, you will be required to discuss it together Note that this consequence—of having to discuss the paper with one's teacher—will likely be enough of a negative consequence to motivate at least some students to not use AI. Many educators do not recommend more severe sanctions for the reasons outlined earlier in this chapter.
By relying on AI, I am handing over my agency and value as a thinking human being to a corporate-controlled algorithm	1. Explain who is financially benefiting from AI 2. Talk about how bypassing critical thought can make you more predictable and more easily manipulated which is a form of intellectual submission

(*Continued*)

Positive Reinforcement Strategies

Anti-GenAI Usage Motivator	*Motivational Strategy*
I want to get positive statements and feedback from my teacher and do really well in this class	1. Cultivate and teach reasoning. Explain to students that rather than traditional grades based on final outputs, you will be looking for evidence of the student's own reasoning during class reflections. Be very positive when students demonstrate genuine examples of good reasoning during discussions 2. Explain and talk about what productive struggle is and its relationship to learning and how sharing it honestly with the class will also be something that you will use as an indicator of learning and success in the class. Bring up and discuss analogies where struggle is necessary and even desirable (though it may not feel good in the moment). Have students think about building muscles when going to the gym, or running to be on a track team, playing a musical instrument, etc. Discuss how the feeling of mastery and accomplishment would be different if such a capability was simply granted and not earned. Consider an Exercise: Think of a time you worked hard for a goal, and got it, how would your experience be different if it was just granted to you?
I want to develop mastery in the skill of (writing, art, publishing, political analysis, song writing, etc.)	1. Explain how one develops mastery in a domain through practice, struggles, overcoming obstacles, over years 2. Show inspiring examples of people that are respected in a field because of their mastery 3. Discuss the difference between that process and asking an AI to do it.
I want to develop my own authentic voice as a writer	1. Explain to students the notion of the authentic voice and the value of cultivating one's true voice and how you will be looking for their unique voice in their writing 2. Show examples of great writers, speakers, intellectuals and inspirational speakers. 3. Demonstrate how relying on an AIs generic voice will detract from one's ability to develop an authentic voice
I want to produce an excellent piece of work that reflects all the time, effort, and thinking I put into it	1. Consider having students engage in a mindfulness strategy to monitor when they are struggling and feeling anxious. That can serve as a reminder to take a deep breath, pause, and remember that discomfort is a *necessary indicator* of their advancement toward creating high-quality work. One good reminder mantra to repeat could be "Productive Struggle" while breathing.

(*Continued*)

Anti-GenAI Usage Motivator	*Motivational Strategy*
I want to be a person of high integrity, acting ethically and of good character	1. Have a class discussion on what it means to be a person of high integrity and good character 2. Ask the class to talk about how this plays out in the use of AI
I want to rise, be respected, accomplished, and succeed in my future career	1. Discuss how, even though AI will almost certainly play some role at one's future workplace, people that truly stand out and excel will embody and have abilities that set them apart from others that may over-rely on AI 2. Share examples of how the human traits of creativity, innovation, empathy, teamwork, and emotional IQ are vital in a workplace and career 3. Bring in an employer and have them share why they need critical thinkers
I want to be a good environmental citizen and play my part in creating a sustainable healthy planet	1. Explain the energy and water use of AI Data centers and impact on environmental issues 2. Demonstrate how energy is used with each AI prompt, and find a yardstick to make a meaningful comparison of energy used for AI and other uses (e.g., how much your town uses in a month, etc.) 3. Engage in a conversation about what it means to care about the environment and how one uses AI.

One note on the negative reinforcements listed above, especially those that relate to brain function degradation that is fear based. Is that fair and appropriate for students? Perhaps. We have all seen public health announcements about matters like the implications of driving while intoxicated, smoking or drug abuse that use frightening messages and images as a motivator. Is this OK in the classroom? Of course it will depend on students' age, maturity, and the technique you choose. So, it will have to be a judgment call used carefully by the educator, and perhaps requiring higher level approvals.

AI Literacy Instruction

Finally, note that another important strategy is to be sure students are taught AI literacy, which ideally, though not necessarily falls under the purview of the librarian, an institution's trained information and research content expert and a neutral, trusted, supportive student resource.

Another reason why librarians are so well suited to teaching AI literacy is that they can help students understand how to see AI as another—albeit powerful and unique—research and analysis tool, with its own strengths and weaknesses, making it appropriate for some tasks and not for others.

And so, just as an information literacy course would explain when to turn to, say a scholarly journal, a news source, a general Google search, a keyword searchable archival database, a book, a data set, a government document, Wikipedia, or any other research source, the instructor should explain the strengths and weaknesses of Generative AI as an information gathering and analysis tool are as well, and help the student understand when using it is not going to produce the best result, and so, their performance, output, and potentially their grade may not be as high either.

Works Cited

Archer-Kuhn, B. (2020). *Inquiry-based learning: A guide for social work educators in higher education Faculty of Social Work*. University of Calgary.

English, M. C., & Kitsantas, A. (2013). Supporting student self-regulated learning in problem- and project-based learning. *Interdisciplinary Journal of Problem-based Learning, 7*(2), 133–137.

Hattie, J. (2009). *Visible learning: A synthesis of over 800 meta-analyses relating to achievement*. Routledge.

Lovett, M. C. (2008, January). Teaching metacognition. In Presentation to the Educause Learning Initiative Annual Meeting. Retrieved on September (Vol. 10, p. 2013).

Nilson, L. B. (2013). *Creating self-regulated learners: Strategies to strengthen students' self-awareness and learning skills*. Stylus Publishing/Routledge.

Nilson, L. B. (2014, June 16). The secret of self-regulated learning. Faculty Focus. https://www.facultyfocus.com/articles/teaching-and-learning/secret-self-regulated-learning/

Pintrich, P. R. (2000). The role of goal orientation in self-regulated learning. In M. Boekaerts, P. R. Pintrich, & M. Zeidner (Eds.), *Handbook of self-regulation* (pp. 451–502). Academic Press/San Diego, CA.

Pope Leo XIV. (2026, May 15). *Magnifica humanitas [Encyclical]*. The Holy See.

Postman, N. (1979). *Teaching as a conserving activity*. Delacorte Press.

Postman, N. (1999). *Building a bridge to the 18th century: How the past can improve our future*. Alfred A. Knop.

Ratnayake, A., Bansal, A., Wong, N., Saseetharan, T., Prompiengchai, S., Jenne, A., Thiagavel, J., & Ashok, A. (2024). All "wrapped" up in reflection: Supporting metacognitive awareness to promote students' self-regulated learning. *Journal of Microbiology & Biology Education, 25*(1), Article e0010323.

Shroff, L. (2026, April 10). *Is schoolwork optional now?* The Atlantic.

Schunk, D. H., & Zimmerman, B. J. (Eds.). (1994). *Self-regulation of learning and performance: Issues and educational applications*. Lawrence Erlbaum Associate.

5 Lessons Learned and Future Forewarnings

Preserving student learning and critical thinking amid pervasive artificial intelligence (AI) requires adaptable educational strategies aligned with individual institutional contexts, active classroom dialogue, transparent ethics, and foundational discussions on the nature of learning. Because final student outputs no longer reliably reflect skill acquisition, assignments must be scaffolded with iterative metacognitive reflections and designed to alter student cost-benefit calculations regarding AI usage.

Rapidly evolving technological developments—including refined educational AI models targeting skill mastery, localized institution-specific chatbots, and autonomous Agentic AI—pose significant challenges to traditional assessment, particularly in online environments. Countering automated cognitive offloading demands making learning visible through synchronous discussions, edit-history tracking, live oral defenses, and process-oriented assessments. Simultaneously, educators must address the subtle risks of Persuasive AI and hyper-personalized model overfitting, which foster fluency bias and obscure illogical reasoning.

Mitigating these cognitive hazards necessitates applying the precautionary principle to safeguard student intellectual development. Beyond technological counter-measures, holistic, experiential, and project-based frameworks offer vital pathways forward. In particular, Indigenous pedagogies center relationality, ethical engagement, and human agency in knowledge creation, reframing the discourse from surveillance and academic dishonesty toward relational integrity, authentic evidence of learning, and human flourishing.

This short book has covered a lot of ground, and as has been noted, not every strategy or approach will work for everyone. Each educator will need to assess their own context, circumstance, priorities, and personal style to determine

DOI: 10.4324/9781003770978-6

which ones make the most sense to try. That said, here are key takeaways most broadly applicable:

Don't ignore this elephant in the classroom-talk about it. Consider coming up with your own personal ethical policy on AI, share it with your students, and help them come up with their own. By doing this you will also create a classroom that is transparent and open.

Consider this advice from Maryellen Weimer, PhD, Professor Emerita, Penn State Berks (Reading, PA): "One of the best gifts teachers can give students are the experiences that open their eyes to themselves as learner" (Weimer, 2014). *Spend the first session or two discussing learning and the relationship of AI to learning and critical thinking. See what you can do to lead students to understand what learning is and why it is so important.*

When creating an assignment, remember that a final output, on its own, is likely no longer a reliable measure of what skills a student developed, how they analyzed a problem, or what they learned. It is now more critical than ever to create assignments that are scaffolded with reflections at key intervals.

Remember too, the cost-benefit that students make when choosing to use AI to complete a class assignment. But you still have the power and option to adjust the external environment, primarily the classroom design, as well as student motivations to change that calculation.

How to Get Started

The biggest obstacles you may have in instituting recommended classroom changes are inertia, time pressures, and the convenience of doing things as they've always been done. And those forces are real and powerful (and not all that dissimilar to why students turn to AI).

But these obstacles can be made less burdensome. You can, for example, start by picking one of the low-hanging fruits from the strategies in this book that feel most aligned to your class and style of teaching. Start slowly, monitor how it goes, and see how it all unfolded-consider an informal post-assignment survey with students for feedback to inform future iterations.

Note: If you are in a position that provides professional development to faculty, pay attention to the findings from a May 2026 AAC&U study (Jacob, 2026) that shared what faculty said they want in a session to make it fit with their workload and therefore more likely to implement. This study consisted of four focus groups of faculty, IT Leaders, administrators, and students, followed by survey results that showed that faculty wanted *shorter and more focused sessions*, even if it just introduced a single tool or idea—not longer and infrequent sessions.

Another finding was that any instructional designers, academic technologists, teaching center staff, and librarians involved in the training should be brought into planning sessions at the beginning to help shape the output, not just included at the end of the process.

Future Trends

The future of AI in education is obviously impossible to exactly foresee, but these key phenomena are already underway.

Producers of Educational AI Models Are Addressing Their Known Flaws

There is, of course, an incentive for producers of Educational AI systems to continually introduce improved models that do not suffer from the kinds of teaching flaws pointed out by educational experts. Most notably, in 2026 Khan Academy, the producer of Khanmigo, the most popular educational AI teaching system, announced that after examining how students were actually using its system, and identifying where it was not optimizing learning as it was hoped, decided to shelve its product and announce a fully revamped one. In its announcement, the company said that drawing on research into help-seeking behavior, the team has differentiated how the AI supports students before and after they attempt a problem. It also adapts based on whether a student is encountering a skill for the first time or reviewing it, and can now prompt a review of prerequisite skills when it detects gaps in mastery.

This reference to "mastery," for example, is certainly a response to studies that have shown that AI *can* be valuable for meaningful learning, but *only* if the student has already mastered the basics of the subject.

Of course, even as newer educational AIs are produced, and address their known flaws, the one thing it will never be able to change is what it is not: it is not a human teacher.

More Effective Educational ChatBots

On the positive side, we might see professors and educational institutions themselves be able to more easily create AI systems designed from the bottom up as educational: these would be trained on the relevant disciplinary and/or class materials and pre-designed to help students understand the subject in sound ways. That was the goal of Northern Arizona Professor of Psychology and Co-Executive Director, Institute for Advancing Applications in Artificial Intelligence, Dr. Michelle Miller when she created her "MillerBot" for her Psychology 101 students. Miller, who told me she generally falls into the "pro-AI" camp, said that it was not that hard for her to generate it either-it was just a matter of taking a Coursera course and using ChatGPT to create her bot.

In my own trials of the bot, which is available for anyone to try at: https://chatgpt.com/g/g-68a250a4b0748191a692475f2da5763a-millerbot, I was quite impressed with its structure and quality as a learning tool. [As a side note, I ran into one academic dilemma when prompting it for knowledge related to psychological motivations for learning. One of the responses, which sounded quite valid based on what I already knew, was "Psychology predicts that most students will offload cognition when given the chance, unless the environment is designed to support the harder choice." Because this statement was the result of the fusion of knowledge from the bot's set of educational materials, there would be no way to truly use that quote—or any other from the bot—as a citation to an original source, other than to the Bot itself, which would seem problematic.]

Agentic AI

As noted in the preface, Agentic AI, or AI agents represent a growing and perhaps even an existential threat to online classes.

IBM defines AI agents as "autonomous AI systems that can independently set goals, plan sequential steps, and take actions using tools to achieve an objective with minimal human supervision. Unlike traditional AI or chatbots that just answer questions, agentic AI actively *does* the work" (https://www.ibm.com/think/topics/agentic-ai For many in business AI agents have provided practical value for offloading repetitive mundane digital tasks and increasing a worker's ability, potentially, to spend time on higher order and more substantive tasks.

Why are these such a threat to online education? The reality is that AI agents can be instructed to, on a predetermined time schedule, log into a student's Learning Management System (LMS), and download current readings, lectures, and assignments. And then, drawing from those materials and the teacher's instructions and rubrics, complete and upload assignments. The entire transaction happens without the student ever needing to have the slightest interaction with the actual classroom. In fact, AI agents can also compose and create a discussion post that responds to what their peers have posted. They can even be instructed to take on the persona of a student and register for a class.

Clearly, this is a very distressing picture, especially as it is not something to worry about in the future but is already happening today (Shroff, 2026). However, despite this ominous state of affairs, most educators that include online classes or teach fully online have options to preserve student learning and thinking in their classes. The key for educators is to determine upfront, before the class begins, what structures or processes to create that will be persuasive *of student learning*.

Like Solving a Murder Mystery

As David Wiley wrote in *Asking a More Productive Question about AI and Assessment* (Wiley, 2025), confronting this quagmire still comes down to the educator asking themselves ahead of time "What kind of evidence could I gather from students that would persuade me that they know the things they need to know at the end of this week / module / course?" Wiley even compares this process to what detectives do when they look for evidence to solve a murder mystery. But, as he noted, in the classroom, AI now "changes evidence that was previously persuasive into evidence that is no longer persuasive" and so continuing the metaphor, he says the existence of AI now "contaminates the crime scene."

Designing an online class so that the students' can demonstrate their learning to the teacher "uncontaminated" by AI may be challenging, but one of the best strategies is to do so by "making learning visible." Consider that several AI-resilient methods described in Chapter 3, the reflective wrappers introduced in Chapter 4, and other approaches outlined earlier can be categorized as making student learning visible.

There are different approaches for making learning visible. Some faculty have their students do their work and maintain all their edit history in a Google Doc or other shared writing platform maintained on the institution's server. In these cases, the professor requires students to use that digital workspace to do all their drafts, updating it with newer versions. Others have the students demonstrate in real time what they learned online.

Michelle Kassorla, one of the educators interviewed in Chapter 3, says that the extent of this problem is very large. She has been working with faculty members around the nation who are interested in resolving this issue. She shared some of her findings with me. For one, she says that one must be aware that anything a student can do with a browser an agent can do with a browser, and it's very hard to identify and stop them. Furthermore, there are literally thousands of agents right now, the most popular ones are browser-based agents like Perplexity's Comet Browser agent and OpenAI's Atlas agent. Other popular browser-based agents include Google's Project Mariner and Anthropic's "Computer Use" agent. In addition, she says there are "tons of independent—non-browser-based-agents like Manus, N8N and Twin, which usually work as a chrome add-on or an app on a computer or phone."

This certainly appears to be a frustratingly maddening challenge. Still, Kassorla says there are ways to deal with it, including:

- **Lockdown browser.** The first approach is to use a lockdown browser. Right now, that currently can shut agents down (but most likely not for long).
- **Curricular and assessment changes.** Kassorla believes that educators must all learn to teach with AI and not against it. It is important to start making some serious changes in what and how we teach what we teach. This is much harder for programs that are carefully controlled by local, state, or federal certification—but for those who are not, these changes are essential.
  - **Formative assessment**—Short, frequent assignments that show learning.
  - **Scaffolded assignments**—One assignment built on the next.

- **Metacognitive reflection**—Asking students to provide in-action and after-action reflection. In-action reflection is done with footnotes (ask for at least five per page) that require the students to talk about the process of their creation. After-action metacognitive reflection asks students to find a greater meaning in what they have accomplished.
- **Transparency statements**—Students must share what AI tools they used and how they used them in the assignment.
- **Shared chatlogs**—Students share the chatlogs created when they complete an AI-infused assignment. Faculty can read these to determine whether the student completed the assignment successfully. Also, students can be asked to annotate these logs to show their process and how they can improve interaction and critical thinking with AI tools.
- **Redesigned rubrics**—Redesign rubrics from grading mechanical processes (like grammar, punctuation, semantics, vocabulary) to consider things like following directions, human voice, agency, clarity, correct facts, and ethical use of AI.

In the end, as with the other strategies provided in this book, each online educator will need to develop their own specific tactics on what is possible to do and what will work best. Among methods to consider:

- Change from teaching asynchronous to a live synchronous course.
- Schedule a weekly live session where students explain what they learned over the past week and how they did it. Cameras must be on and questions should be asked by the professor in front of the rest of the class.
- If there was an exam in the course the student had to previously upload, make their learning visible, and require the student to appear live to discuss their work or have them explain their thinking and reasoning from a few questions randomly chosen by the instructor; or conduct the exam itself live online.
- Ensure the course syllabus specifically outlines your expectations about AI and that any use of Agentic AI is considered a major violation of academic integrity. This should be stated directly to the class early on in the course.

What about really large online classes, those with hundreds of students? The above strategies are much more difficult to implement as a single professor, or even one with a couple of TAs, won't be able to handle the workload involved for holding live sessions or even monitoring students' learning process. So, it is here that the really hard decisions have to be faced. Some educators have argued that the inability to effectively guarantee learning in these very large online classes just points out their already existing weaknesses and their value and so their life should come to an end. However, the problem is that these classes were specifically created to provide educational opportunities for those who for a variety of real reasons—disability, distance, travel, military, family obligations, and so on—simply cannot attend an in-person class.

This is not an easy problem to solve for these very large online classes. One suggestion has been to deploy an AI avatar to query students live. Given that the technological imperative seems to prevail so often, this may become a mainstream solution. But no doubt this will raise perhaps even more fundamental issues in teaching and learning.

To learn more about Agentic AI, Kassorla recommends this online guide, the "Higher Ed Professionals Guide to Agentic AI." Available at https://bit.ly/4dPdnxN.

Persuasive AI

In December 2024, the Computing Community Consortium (CCC), whose mission is to "enable the pursuit of innovative, high-impact computing research that aligns with pressing national and global challenges" published *Future of Information Retrieval Research in the Age of AI* (Allan, 2024). In section 4.4.1b, "The AI Persuasion Mechanism," researchers reported on their concerns that GenAI could be used to inappropriately persuade a user to accept a belief or course of action. This study explains, "... generative systems may inadvertently (or intentionally) persuade users on opinions or perspectives that they do not already hold—for example, by masquerading as a trustworthy source or appealing to learned biases of the user."

In one sense, all Large Language Model AIs can be thought of as persuasive, as they produce text to inform and convince the user of their answers and analyses. But Persuasive AI, can be hyper personalized and produced with the precise mission to persuade a targeted small cohort or even a single individual with malicious intent, tailoring its output to what it has calculated to be the most effective means of persuading based on what it already knows about that target.

It's also worth noting that under Section 4.5, "Personalization": the report makes this disturbing prediction: "While traditional IR [information retrieval] can return what exists, future IR systems will generate what you want even if it doesn't exist (or a process for making it)."

While malicious targeted Persuasive AI isn't likely to infiltrate all the way down to edtech or AI-generated lesson plans, it is not beyond imagining the possibility. At a minimum, the existence of Persuasive AI should at least be addressed as part of AI literacy instruction. It can be taught as something a student should be on guard for when they venture onto the publicly available open AI systems, especially when researching contentious political and social issues.

Another problem likely to increase as time goes on is a different form of misinformation that has not received much attention: AI's tendency to *overfit* answers when it personalizes its response. This can occur when AI knows who a particular user is (knowing because the person subscribed to the product, or they enabled personalization features). The AI system can retain a history of that user's past queries and projects. By analyzing this data, the AI can and will make determinations about what the person has been working on, what they are trying to discover, and even what kind of person they are (age, views, concerns, etc., based on previous prompts).

Sometimes having this context makes the AI's responses more relevant and useful. But what also may happen is that the AI "tries too hard" to make these newer questions and topics somehow fit "logically" into its larger schema of what it *assumes* a particular user wants, even when those new queries and topics are completely unrelated to that user's previous ones. This can cause the AI to force a connection between unrelated concepts and produce illogical and irrelevant analyses that may sound convincing but are actually illogical or even nonsensical with faulty analyses. This can be more problematic than errors in fact, as those can at least be checked, but because we have a tendency to trust information that *sounds* clear and articulated smoothly ("fluency bias"), we can easily be led astray. As AI companies increasingly try to make their systems more personalized, this problem is likely to increase over time.

Changing How We Think and Reason

In *The Age of AI and our Human Future*, Erich Schmidt, previous CEO of Google, Daniel Huttenlocher, Dean of the Schwarzman College of Computing at MIT, and the late Henry Kissinger examine how, over history, humans relied on a variety of methods to analyze the world and understand reality: early on there was superstition, faith, and with the Enlightenment rational reasoning, calling upon: thinking, logic, deduction, and analysis. (Kissinger, 2021)

But as the authors note, AI "figures out the world" very differently. It does so through drawing from its massive data collection, enormous computing power, the deployment of natural language processing tasks to mimic human speech, and its use of probability to identify the most meaningful connections between its data. Some do argue that this process is another *form* of reasoning–but it is still not the same process that humans take to understand the world.

As AI continues to improve rapidly, it becomes clearer that, in an increasing number of domains and problems, it will prove to be a superior method (i.e., more likely to be accurate and faster) for surfacing important hidden knowledge. The authors posit there may well come a time, when individuals and institutions make what seems like a rational decision to choose to *defer their reason*ing to AI. The essential question becomes: how does this change who we all are, and for young people and students, how does it change the way they learn to figure out their world?

The Precautionary Principle

For the immediate moment what is most important to consider is the element of *risk* that AI presents, specifically to student learning and their critical thinking development. The precautionary principle was created to lead decision-makers to adopt precautionary measures when scientific evidence about an environmental or human health hazard was uncertain and when the stakes are high. This principle should be applied to the probable cognitive health hazard of AI damaging the development of critical thinking in young people. Certainly, the stakes of what could be lost are extremely high.

Research is underway to dig deep and rigorously into not just how often students use AI, but what they are doing, and what remedies that have been put into play are actually showing promise. For example, in a conversation with Susanna Loeb, Professor at the Graduate School of Education, and *Faculty Director, SCALE Initiative* at Stanford University, she told me that in a partnership with an initiative at the University of Tartu (Tartu, Finland) her group is researching not just *how often* students use AI or under what conditions, but the *content of their interactions*. She said,

> We are getting access to what students actually write in their Large Language Models (LLMs). For researchers at the University of Tartu, they can look at the data as it comes in and see exactly what students type. Does it appear to be cognitive offloading? I only care about "cheating" to the point where it hinders student development. We want to measure if they are developing curiosity, critical thinking, and engagement.

There is no downside in taking the actions that the precautionary principle would advise in order to save and preserve critical thinking. In fact, choosing to implement measures that educational experts know work for cultivating student learning and thinking will produce something every teacher, professor, librarian, parent, and citizen would want: a more engaged, skilled youth who are developing learning and critical thinking skills and will apply them throughout their lives.

One Final Thought

The uncertain future we currently face is a motivator to continue efforts to create new and innovative methods for facilitating student learning and critical skills development. In addition to the innovative efforts now underway as described in this book, it is important to remember there are many ways critical thinking can be developed. These include experiential learning (employed by the well-known Waldorf schools), project-based learning, hands-on, and object-based learning to name a few. And science education integrates physical experimental work, observations, and analysis as well of course. Moving into the future, these and other more physical and holistic types of learning assignments may become increasingly important.

An important education perspective that needs to be seriously listened to and given space in our critical thinking development toolkit going forward is the Indigenous approach to learning.

Highlighting the profound dimension of Indigenous learning perspectives and how it is being applied to the impacts of AI on student thinking processes, Dr. Gregory Sutherland, a Métis educator and lecturer in Indigenous pedagogies and practice at Simon Fraser University, British Columbia, Canada, in a recent article, explored the relationship of GenAI to Indigenous ways of knowing. He observes that

> Indigenous knowledge systems recognize the self as part of the process of learning and understanding, whereas GenAI prevents users from honouring themselves as participants in knowledge creation. Who we are and what experiences we bring to learning shapes how we understand the world. If users allow the work of meaning-making to be done by GenAI, no real learning is occurring… the tenets of Indigenous education can help us to reframe the discourse around GenAI from one of surveillance, academic dishonesty, and appropriation, to one that is about relationships, ethicality, and respect.
>
> (Sutherland, 2024)

Given the uncertainty of our times, perhaps it is fitting to conclude this book with a question. It was posed in the Indigenous Protocol and Artificial Intelligence Position Paper (Lewis, 2020). To answer it requires the application of critical thinking filtered through the lens of Indigenous values and paradigms, and that is: "*How do we imagine a future with AI that contributes to the flourishing of all humans and non-humans?*"

Works Cited

Allan, J., Choi, E., Lopresti, D., & Zamani, H. (2024). *Future of information retrieval research in the age of generative AI CCC workshop report*. Washington, DC: Computing Research Association (CRA). https://doi.org/10.48550/arXiv.2412.02043

Jacob, S., Miceli, H., Schneider, H., & Peters Hinton, V. (2026, May). *Institutional conditions for integrating emerging technologies in higher education*. Digital Promise. https://doi.org/10.51388/20.500.12265/294

Kissinger, H. A., Schmidt, E., & Huttenlocher, D. (2021). *The age of AI and our human future*. Little, Brown and Company.

Lewis, J. E. (Ed.). (2020). *Indigenous protocol and artificial intelligence position paper*. The Initiative for Indigenous Futures and the Canadian Institute for Advanced Research.

Shroff, L. (2026, April 10). *Is schoolwork optional now?* The Atlantic.

Sutherland, G. (2024, December/January). Understanding GenAI through Indigenous ways of knowing. *BCTF Teacher: Magazine of the BC Teachers' Federation, 37*(3).

Weimer, M. (2014, November 12). *Prompts to help students reflect on how they approach learning*. The Teaching Professor.

Wiley, D. (2025). Asking a more productive question about AI and assessment. *TechTrends, 69*, 864–865. https://doi.org/10.1007/s11528-025-01118-5

Appendix

Government Policy Guidance for Classroom AI

This appendix briefly outlines several leading country and regional initiatives to illustrate countries leading in addressing the challenges of AI in education. National programs addressing AI in the classroom can generally be grouped into three broad categories: laws and regulations; guidance and resources; and educational programs (AI literacy).

Laws and Regulations

Few countries have passed laws restricting how AI is allowed to be used in the classroom. There are, though, a few notable examples, as follows:

EU – The EU's 2024 AI Act covers a much broader expanse than education in how AI may or may not be used; however, education falls into a category of AI use called "high-risk," and so the law does ban one specific use of AI in the classroom, which is to use it to detect student emotional state in any way.

United States – While there are no specific national laws in the United States on AI in the classroom, California was the first US state to pass legislation requiring the teaching of students (in secondary school) how to understand AI, that is, getting instruction in AI literacy (AB 2876 enacted on September 9, 2024).

China – the Chinese Ministry of Education published its *Guide to Using Generative Artificial Intelligence in Primary and Secondary School* (May 2025). This document includes both prohibitions and guidance. Below is a segment that specifically relates to critical thinking and learning in the classroom:

> ... *"teachers shall not use GenAI as a substitute for teaching and are prohibited from directly using AI to answer students' questions or provide consultation and that they "shall avoid directly using AI-generated content to evaluate students"... teachers that it can "use GenAI as a supplementary tool in assessment system design, strengthen human review and critical judgement, and put an end to the direct use of AI outputs as assessment conclusion."*

The complete English version can be accessed at: https://cset.georgetown.edu/publication/china-education-powerhouse-plan-2024-2035/

Guidance and Resources

Rather than passing laws and regulations, it is much more common for countries to provide guidance and resources for educators to address AI in the classroom. Here are some examples:

Australia—the *Australian Framework for Generative AI* in Schools (2025) offers guidance for educators on the efficacious and ethical use of AI in the classroom.

https://www.education.gov.au/schooling/resources/australian-framework-generative-artificial-intelligence-ai-schools

EU—the *Framework for the Educational Use of Generative Artificial Intelligence in the European Schools* in 2025 established that "Generative AI tools are approached and used to support and enhance critical thinking and creativity rather than restrict human thought and experience." Further, in March 2026, the EU published its updated *Guidelines on the Ethical Use of Artificial Intelligence and Data in Teaching and Learning for Educators.*

Denmark—announced its mission to upskill 1 million people with AI literacy skills by 2028 through its *AI Competence Pact.*

Ireland—created an *AI in Schools External Taskforce* in October 2025, which, through structured forums and its publication, *Guidance on Artificial Intelligence (AI) in Schools*, was created to assist educators in integrating AI into their teaching and learning. The country also made educational resources available on its Department of Education Support and Advice site, which included case studies of teachers who applied best practices in their use of AI.

Italy—has published its Guidelines for the Introduction of Artificial Intelligence in Schools, which covers topics such as the role of AI in schools, ethical requirements, personal data protection, and risk mitigation.

Taiwan -through its *AI for ALL* initiative, in 2023, announced it was committed to introducing an AI Curriculum to over 4,400 teachers and 300,000 students across the country within three years. Its larger mission included informing policy, guidance, and support for AI in education and improving knowledge of AI among teachers and students, especially in rural and underserved communities. The program also provides structured instruction and self-guided problem-solving to avoid the risks of "AI-induced skill atrophy," avoiding a decline in student critical thinking and judgment.

Singapore—The country's Ministry of Education has made available access to its Singapore Student Learning Space (SLS), a national online platform for teaching and learning that provides "pedagogically sound AI tools with [built-in] safety guardrails." One of the tools is its Learning Assistant (LEA) that "helps students learn by asking guiding questions." A full teachers' guide on how to use LEA is also available: https://bit.ly/3S6Q8bk

China—In addition to its laws noted above, China also provides general guidance and recommendations both to educators and to students:

> For educators. Under student ability evaluation, the report directed teachers to *focus on higher-order thinking dimensions such as creativity and critical thinking that AI cannot replace and revise existing evaluation schemes accordingly...*
>
> For students. The document says that students should... *learn to use GenAI critically, strictly adhere to norms of academic integrity, enhance their awareness of privacy and security, and achieve comprehensive development of core competencies. ...avoid abusing GenAI in learning tasks that require creative or personalized expression, thus losing individual thought and perspective; avoid rashly using GenAI to obtain information without first consulting high-quality textbooks or authoritative sources..."*
>
> Under Scenario 2: Providing interactive exploration, China also lists its "encouraged student uses." *Here the report advises that "students can use interactive exploration environments built with GenAI technology to engage in interactive learning practices and systematically improve their logical reasoning, critical thinking and innovative thinking. For example, students can: Analyze complex issues such as climate change and cultural heritage through cross-disciplinary knowledge maps, obtain intelligent suggestions and data analysis frameworks using natural language interaction, dynamically adjust parameters in their simulation experiments, generate visual models and issue risk warnings; use virtual reality (VR) technology to achieve three-dimensional reconstructions of historical events and micro-processes, support hypothesis testing and system cognition construction; simulate innovative solutions such as smart city design in AI sandboxes..."*

AI Literacy Initiatives

AI literacy programs are growing rapidly around the globe. These instructional sessions typically include lessons on demystifying how AI works, algorithmic awareness, producing effective prompts, and how to critically analyze AI-generated content for errors and bias, and how to identify synthetic text and deepfakes.

Below is a brief summary of regional bodies and individual countries that have made early strides in rolling out AI literacy nationwide.

European Commission—In May 2025, the OECD and the European Commission, in partnership with Code.org and TeachAI, published its *Global AI Literacy Framework: Empowering Learners for the Age of AI*. Its aim is to empower learners to understand AI and make meaningful and ethical decisions about its use.

Ireland—created its *Guidance on Artificial Intelligence in Schools* (2025) which complements its revised National AI Strategy (2024) by providing education-specific principles for responsible GenAI use.

Uruguay—updated its "Plan Ceibal," first launched in 2007, to include a new pedagogical framework that includes AI education in the school curricula, with a focus on critical thinking, problem-solving, creativity, and collaboration.

Dubai—On February 26, 2026, at the World Governments Summit 2026, Dubai announced that it was launching a major AI literacy initiative with a goal of providing AI literacy to 3,600 teachers and approximately 80,500 students in a program that will run through February 2030. The programme will include professional development, tools, and assessment guidance on how to deliver AI learning across designated core subjects.

USA—the US Department of Education published several informative reports and papers on its recommended uses and cautions in using AI in the classroom. Most notable is its comprehensive study, *Artificial Intelligence and the Future of Teaching and Learning* (US Department of Education, 2023).

Other National Initiatives

Below is a briefer summary from the OECD of what a wider range of countries as well as two major international bodies are doing to address AI in schools (OECD, 2026):

Australia: the Framework for Generative Artificial Intelligence in Schools highlights six principles, including diversity of perspectives, non-discrimination, privacy and data protection, and human oversight. Unlike earlier AI strategies, it addresses classroom uses of text- and image-generating systems.

Japan: the government provides guidance on generative AI (GenAI) in schools that explicitly warns against inputting personal or sensitive data into GenAI systems, reflecting early recognition of LLM-specific data reuse and retraining risks in education.

United Kingdom (Wales): the document on Generative artificial intelligence in education is explicitly focused on the use of GenAI, complemented by guidance addressing AI-specific risks such as deepfakes and synthetic media.

Finland: the Finnish National Agency for Education issued its Recommendations on the Use of Artificial Intelligence in Education, covering both practical guidance and policy reference for GenAI.

France: the Cadre d'usage de l'intelligence artificielle en éducation (2025) (Framework on the use of AI in education) clarifies permitted uses of GenAI in school and sets conditions related to data protection, transparency, and pedagogical responsibility.

Latvia: the Guidelines for the Use of AI in Primary and Secondary Education explicitly address generative tools and critical thinking.

Lithuania: has been preparing recommendations for the Safe Implementation of Artificial Intelligence.

Luxembourg: The KI Kompass (AI Compass) serves as a national reference framework combining views on strategic orientation, pedagogical practice, and professional exchange.

The Netherlands: has produced its Vision on Generative Artificial Intelligence (2024), followed by the Dutch Digitalisation Strategy—Accelerating Together (2025) which provides a cross-sectoral strategy, while education-specific guidance is provided by Kennisnet through the Guide to AI in Education and School Agreements on the Use of Generative AI.

Norway: the Strategy for Digital Competence and Infrastructure in Early Childhood Education and Schools addresses GenAI and is accompanied by national guidelines and competency development packages.

Slovakia: the Strategic Plan for the Integration of Artificial Intelligence into Education includes dedicated initiatives on AI assistants for teachers and personalized learning tools.

Spain: the Guide on the Use of Artificial Intelligence in Education (2024) covers GenAI among other AI tools, for example, to discourage the use of non-compliant generative tools.

Turkey: the Artificial Intelligence in Education Policy Document and Action Plan 2025–2029 explicitly covers the use and access of GenAI alongside ethics and capacity-building considerations.

International Organizations

UNESCO: released in 2024 and 2025 guidance on the adoption of GenAI in education (Guidance for Generative AI in Education and Research, 2025) as well as advice more targeted toward teachers (AI competency framework for teachers, 2024).

UNICEF: in December 2025, UNICEF updated its guidance on AI and children to respond to rapid technological advances like GenAI and new concerns such as AI-generated harmful content. The framework outlines ten principles to ensure AI technologies are safe and supportive of child wellbeing.

Lessons from the Leading Media Literate Countries

Providing national guidance on AI for educators is very new, and it is too early to find out how they are working and measuring success. But some clues can be found by examining past and recent programs introduced by countries who have successfully addressed *media literacy* instruction for their students and citizens. While media literacy is not the same as AI literacy, there are areas of overlap, and so lessons about what it may mean to successfully introduce AI literacy programs may be learned from countries who became leaders in how they became a top-ranked country in media literacy.

So first, how are leaders identified? There are a few reputable global organizations that rank countries in how they score in media literacy. One of the best-known of these rankings is published yearly by the Open Society Institute, which each year uses a set of criteria to determine which countries rank highest. According to the Open Society Institute's 2026 Media Literacy Index (Open Society, 2026), the following countries scored highest in media literacy. They are categorized into "Tier 1" and "Tier 2" countries:

Tier 1: Finland, Denmark, Ireland, the Netherlands, Norway, Switzerland, and Estonia

Tier 2: Canada, Taiwan, Germany, France, England, and Italy

One way to learn AI literacy lessons from these leading media literate countries is to review policies, practices, and priorities these leaders had in common. And of course, it is first necessary to note that while many of their strategies *are* replicable by other countries, some will be more natural outgrowths of embedded values and practices, so tightly woven into their culture and history that they can't be simply replicated and expected to work elsewhere.

For example, Estonia, which consistently ranks toward the top in media literacy (as well as in PISA scores), has a very high culturally embedded value of the importance of knowledge. And Denmark, Norway, and Switzerland, who also consistently rank at the top in media literacy, also have the highest levels of social trust between citizens and from citizens toward their government.

Other countries recognized the value of media and digital literacy skills as a vital security matter. Here they were seen as a bulwark against citizens becoming susceptible to disinformation from aggressor nations who would flood a country's social networks with digital propaganda (now even more powerful when AI-generated) to confuse, mislead, or disrupt the population. Finland and Estonia, as well as Sweden and the Baltic states, have that urgency, and leaders have made digital information literacy a national security imperative to counter digital disinformation initiatives from Russia.

Transferrable Strategies

Despite those special cultural conditions that paved the way for certain countries to develop such high media literacy, there still remain certain practices in common that could likely be adopted by many other countries. These practices can be considered by other educational policy makers and administrators when considering how to make their students (and population) more AI literate. Those practices include:

- Creating a Robust Infrastructure Early on
  Countries that take media literacy seriously start early. Finland, Denmark, Ireland, Norway, Canada, and Taiwan all have students learn those skills in primary school (for Finland, it starts in pre-school).
- Weaving Media Literacy Practices into Existing Courses
  Another clear theme is that these leading countries have not prioritized creating standalone media and technology literacy courses; instead, they integrate those capabilities into the standard courses in the curriculum, such as social studies, English, science, and math. The assumption is that by introducing the skills this way, these literacies will become a repeated skill, with a more meaningful practical context, and be more sustainable over time.
  [Note: despite the value of embedding these skills into existing courses, at the same time, there is an increasing number of critical standalone AI literacy courses being offered by librarians, a vital part of the solution, especially for research purposes.]
- Investment in Professional Teacher Development
  There's no way to effectively provide media, information, or AI literacy skills if the instructors are not knowledgeable in it themselves and trained in how to teach it. Finland and Denmark, among other countries, make sure that teacher professional development and necessary funding are a priority. France has established a teacher training initiative as part of its Center for Media and Information Literacy (CLEMI), part of the country's Réseau Canopé (Ministry of Education).
- Public Resources, Awareness, and Messaging
  These leading countries have also made an effort to produce informative resources and promote awareness programs—not only to educators but to all citizens. These include national fact-checking networks in Estonia, Finland, Norway, and Taiwan; resource guides for using AI in classrooms, created by Finland and Ireland; and age-specific AI usage manuals made available to schools in Taiwan. And while still in formation, in 2019 Canada created its Digital Citizen Research Program, which, according to the government, will "help Canadians understand online disinformation and its impact on Canadian society, and to build the evidence base that will be used to identify possible actions and future policymaking in this space."

Works Cited

Chounta, I.-A. (2026, March). *Artificial intelligence in classrooms: Cognitive dimensions* (Briefing PE 784.575). *Policy Department for Citizens' Rights and Constitutional Affairs, European Parliament.*

European Commission, Directorate-General for Education, Youth, Sport and Culture. (2026). *Guidelines on the ethical use of artificial intelligence and data in teaching and learning for educators*. Publications Office of the European Union.

Open Society Institute – Sofia. (2026, January). *Media Literacy Index 2026: Denmark, Finland, Ireland, and Netherlands lead European ranking of resilience against disinformation*.

U.S. Department of Education, Office of Educational Technology. (2023). *Artificial intelligence and the future of teaching and learning: Insights and recommendations*.

Index

For Product Safety Concerns and Information please contact our EU representative GPSR@taylorandfrancis.com Taylor & Francis Verlag GmbH, Kaufingerstraße 24, 80331 München, Germany